ISLE OF WIGHT VILLAINS

ROGUES, RASCALS AND REPROBATES

T0346948

ISLE OF WIGHT VILLAINS

ROGUES, RASCALS AND REPROBATES

JAN TOMS

First published 2012

The History Press
The Mill, Brimscombe Port
Stroud, Gloucestershire, GL5 2QG
www.thehistorypress.co.uk

Reprinted 2017

© Jan Toms, 2012

The right of Jan Toms to be identified as the Author
of this work has been asserted in accordance with the
Copyrights, Designs and Patents Act 1988.

British Library Cataloguing in Publication Data.
A catalogue record for this book is available from the British Library.

ISBN 978 0 7524 6219 6

Typesetting and origination by The History Press
Printed in Great Britain by TJ Books Ltd, Padstow, Cornwall

Contents

Acknowledgements

I owe a debt of gratitude to the following people and organisations for their generosity in sharing knowledge: the Isle of Wight Public Record Office for unfailing willingness to provide records and information; the Isle of Wight Family History Society for making records of births, deaths and marriages so easily available; Cowes Customs for the huge amount of information supplied on their site www.cowescustoms.co.uk; Mr Alan Champion and Mrs Ann Barratt for sharing a wealth of information online; the Governor at Parkhurst Prison for permitting photography; Mr Robert Hampton for producing the thoroughly enjoyable illustrations for this book; the *Isle of Wight County Press* for unlimited access to their past editions; and Mr Terry Toms for providing support and chauffeuring services, and generally for being there.

Introduction

I am fortunate in having only a passing acquaintance with villainy. When my father was a boy, he was up in court for 'scrumping' apples in Shanklin, but escaped with a telling off. Thankfully, his misdemeanour occurred long after the time when lads were transported to Australia – or my own history might have been very different.

The Island was never a crime capital, although in terms of smuggling it was once in the Premier League. Everything from brandy to tea found its way ashore, and, in the fight against the practice, unhappy revenue men risked their lives and faced hostility from the public.

Murders were rare, thankfully, and on one occasion the Island congratulated itself on existing for sixty years without a single homicide.

In medieval times, there was an upsurge in knife crime; within fourteen years (1377 to 1391), seventeen men were committed for fatal stabbings. Most of these criminals simply ran away, and their fates were not recorded.

The struggle for law and order continued; in 1862, William Thomas was accused of stealing a pebble from his master at Newchurch – for which he was sentenced to three months in gaol. In a terrible example of juvenile delinquency, a young lad crept up behind Miss Phoebe Plaister, headmistress of Bettesworth Road Board School at Ryde, and threw the hood of her cloak over her head before running away. Such behaviour scandalised the neighbourhood.

For centuries, the military was on the Island in large numbers, adding to the incidents of drunkenness, rioting, rape and murder. In the ten months that 1,500 Scotsmen were billeted across the Island during the sixteenth century, they left behind at least seventy illegitimate children.

The conversion of the Parkhurst Military Hospital to a prison saw a series of escapes, filling the locals with trepidation, although nearly every break-out resulted in a swift recapture. Between them, the prison officials and Queen Victoria put the Isle of Wight on the map – although for rather different reasons.

The Island, with its 60-mile coastline, still feels a safe place to live – and long may that last. Though, it is also true that locals and visitors enjoy stories of murder and mayhem from the Island's past...

Jan Toms, 2012

Chapter One

Home-Grown Baddies: Murder, Burglary and Theft

Being a law-abiding place, when a murder is committed on the Island it causes shock and disbelief for years to come. This may explain why the most notorious murder, which took place in 1736, still remains a part of local folklore...

The Gory Story of Michal Morey

Michal Morey was a woodsman growing up at 'Sullens', a lonely cottage in a valley between Newport and Arreton. Even by eighteenth-century standards it was remote. His circumstances would have been familiar to many: little (if any) education, starting work at a young age, marriage, a growing family, and struggling to put food on the table. After Michal's parents died, he remained in the family home, married and had several children. Then, in 1722, another all-too-common tragedy struck the family: his eldest daughter Mary died in childbirth.

At this sad time, she and her husband, Thomas Dove, had been living with Michal. Mary was buried at St George's Church, Arreton, and the motherless child was baptised; he was given the name James.

For several years, Thomas Dove remained with his father-in-law, but then he met another woman and left to set up home with her, leaving James behind. Whether he made any financial arrangement for the boy's care is not recorded, but by this time Michal was fifty-seven and the burden of a grandchild to rear was, no doubt, a great strain on him. For several years, however, grandfather and grandson remained under the same roof, although how they got on is a matter of conjecture.

What happened next is a mystery. In July 1736, Michal, accompanied by his grandson, took a billhook (a curved metal tool used for cutting trees) and two leather satchels, and set off for the nearby woods. Only later was it discovered that the old man struck the boy so violently with the billhook that he nearly severed his head. He then dismembered the body and hid the pieces in the satchels somewhere in the woods.

It seems that, initially, Michal returned home, and when asked about James' whereabouts, he was vague. His demeanour gave rise to suspicion and, when pressurised about James, he in turn disappeared. The hue and cry (a legal requirement dating from at the least the thirteenth century) was raised, calling on the local citizens to join the search for this suspected felon. At Newport, a reward of 2 guineas was offered for his capture, and the countryside was scoured to find him. Michal, who had been hiding – allegedly in a cave – eventually returned home, but when a search of his house was undertaken, his bloodstained shirt was discovered. He was detained on the suspicion of James' murder and held in custody at Winchester Gaol.

A further reward was offered to whoever could find James; it was several weeks before his decomposing body was discovered. The 2 guineas went to local man, Richard Norris. A hasty court was assembled and the gruesome, mutilated remains of James left no doubt as to how he had met his end.

In his book *For Rooks and Ravens*, Kenneth S. Phillips describes the ghastly moment when the satchels were opened: 'The head, shoes and a sea of maggots rolled on to the grass…' In the end, James was identified only by his clothes. His burial was hastily arranged in Arreton churchyard.

The body of James Dove is discovered.

Michael spent seven months in custody at Winchester before his trial. While he was in gaol, his son Richard gave him money supplied by the parish. The parish also bore the cost of the investigation, the inquest, and supplying witnesses; this totalled £36 5s 2d.

Michal never confessed to the murder. The trial was short – an open and shut case – and on 19 March 1737 he was tried, found guilty and publicly executed within an hour. His body was then encased in a metal frame and returned to the Island to hang in chains near the crossroads at Arreton village – a grim warning to other would be wrongdoers. There it remained, pecked by crows and slowly rotting on the Bronze-Age burial mound still known as Michal Morey's Hump. Local man John Phillips was paid £6 5s for making a gibbet from which to suspend him.

A few ghoulish mementoes of this incident are said to remain. Some of the wood from the gibbet was allegedly used in the construction of the snug at the adjacent pub, the Hare and Hounds, and several skulls, believed to be of Anglo-Saxon origin, were later unearthed at the hump; one, believed to be that of Michal Morey, was displayed inside the same pub. Also, at the time that Michal's rotted corpse was taken down for burial, local landowner William Jolliffe is said to have bought the iron frame in which he hung, and had part of it converted into a pipe rack.

In 1737, in the 'Monthly Chronologer' section of the *Gentleman's Monthly Intelligencer* magazine, a laconic report of the country's capital murder cases included 'an old fellow of the Isle of Wight for the murder of his grandson'. Michal, then, became a part of recorded history – an honour he might well have preferred to do without.

A Sorry Tale of Fratricide, Greed and Loss

It seems strange to think that Arreton, an ancient and still unspoilt country village, should be the murder capital of the Isle of Wight. Even before the Morey murder, however, Arreton was the site of a brutal double killing by a scheming son.

In the early sixteenth century, Mr John Leigh, a Wiltshire man, acquired the lease of Arreton Manor, and by the time of his death he was certainly the wealthiest man on the Island. He had two daughters and three sons: John, Edward and Barnaby.

On John senior's death, the manor passed to his first son, John, who died childless, leaving the lease of the manor to his wife Elizabeth, with £20 each to his brothers Edward and Barnaby. When Elizabeth died, it was the third son, Barnaby, who inherited the estate.

John Leigh hurries his father to his grave.

It seems, though, that Barnaby's family was not a happy one and when he in turn lay dying, his thirteen-year-old son, John, anxious to hurry his father to the grave, smothered him by placing a pillow over his face. Tragically, his young sister Annabelle, who was about eight years of age, witnessed this crime. To protect himself, John Leigh dragged Annabelle to an upstairs window and threw her to her death.

This grim episode was not the end of the family's misfortunes. Barnaby's unhappy widow had two brothers, James and Thomas, who both claimed a right to inherit her estate. To settle the matter they fought a duel, during which one brother died instantly and the other followed him a few days later after sustaining serious injury. Thus ended the Leigh's association with Arreton Manor.

Medieval Murder

When somebody was murdered in medieval times, it was up to the coroner – as a servant of the crown – to investigate. The coroner, whose office goes back at least 800 years, was only concerned with establishing whether the court could confiscate any goods or chattels belonging to the attacker. For this reason, the details recorded in his book were about whether the guilty party had any assets and whether he had run away or would agree to leave the country – in which case his belongings could be seized. What ultimately became of the criminal did not interest the court.

There was a particular significance attached to the value of the weapon that had inflicted the fatal damage, whether it were a knife, a gun, a horse or a runaway cart. It was known as a *deodand*, and the original intention was to assess its worth and to give its value to God, to be used in a good cause.

Knife Crime

Of the twenty cases of murder examined by the coroner between 1377 and 1391, seventeen involved knives. Given that the Island's population in 1377 was listed as 4,733, this would seem to be a major cause for concern. Other murder weapons listed were a shovel, a pole and a bottle.

The sorts of knives in general usage at the time were variously known as baselards (a two-edged implement) or, more commonly employed, a 'whittle' (also called a 'thwittle'). A whittle was a type of single-edged blade, commonly carried by working men.

Some Early Cases Recorded by the Coroner

In 1380, John Brigges attacked and killed John Stonelether by hitting him on the head with a baselard at Carisbrooke Mill. As Brigges had nothing of value, his fate is not recorded.

At Mottistone in 1381, John Hardy attacked William Gugge with his thwittle, stabbing him in the stomach. Hardy took flight, and at the inquest his goods were valued a £1 16s. The knife was valued at 1d.

In 1382, John Milward attacked John Dawe with his thwittle, causing a 5in wound from which Dawe died. At the inquest at Carisbrooke, it was recorded that Dawe had fled and possessed no goods. His knife was valued at 2d.

Three Cases of Self-Defence?

In 1377, in a field near Ryde, John Aleyn and John Grontale got into a fight. Aleyn was thrown to the ground and Grontale came at him with a knife. Drawing his own knife to protect himself, it seems that in the struggle Aleyn fell on it and died from the wound. The offending knife was valued at 4s. Aleyn's goods were worth £2.

In 1379 at Kern, on the outskirts of Brading, Walter Pedder attacked John Hawkyn twice with a thwittle. It was an unprovoked assault and John drew his own knife and struck out, penetrating Pedder's arm. He died from the wound. As John Hawkyn had acted in self-defence, it was Pedder's goods that were forfeited, being valued at 10s.

The year 1383 saw Robert Gilberd kill John Underwode by stabbing him. He claimed self-defence. The event happened in Sandown; after shouting insults at each other, John struck Robert twice and Robert retaliated with his dagger. John had no possessions to confiscate. The dagger was valued at 2d.

I Blame the Non-Conformists

On 21 June 1812, Mr Hill, shoemaker of Shalfleet, and his son attended church. While they were away, his wife Elizabeth was brutally hacked to death with a hatchet by her husband's apprentice, nineteen-year-old John James.

John had grown up in the village and, apparently, was well-treated and at all times; he had been considered 'normal'. When accused of the crime, he readily admitted his guilt but could offer no explanation as to why he had done it. He further declared that had anyone else been at home at the time, he would have killed them too.

On being cross-examined, he referred to a biblical text from the Book of Job, in which the writer longs for a place that is described as follows: 'The small and the great are there; and the servant is free of the master.'

At his trial, James was expressionless and silent. The *Oxford Journal* of 18 July 1812 described him as being in a state of melancholic apathy. The judge, Sir Alan Chambre, concluded that he was an 'enthusiastic Methodist' and condemned the dangerous effects of 'vulgar and literal constructions of scriptural passages'.

In the face of overwhelming evidence, John James was found guilty and hanged the following day, 'after spending a considerable time in devotion'. His body was then handed over to the hospital for dissection.

Here Comes the Candle

Citizens of Ryde awoke on the morning of 10 December 1863 to the shocking news that at a small cottage in Cullimore Yard, off St John's Road, a young woman had been murdered. Those who knew the perpetrator, Robert Hallett, might well have shaken their heads and said, 'I always knew that he would come to a bad end.'

Hallett came from a respectable family but was the archetypal 'black sheep'. He was widely blamed for the early death of his wife, who had succumbed under the pressure of his drinking and whoring. She left behind a ten-year-old son. Also, only recently had Hallett assaulted his neighbour.

The murder victim was Mary Anne Phillips, rather snootily referred to in the press as the 'paramour' of Hallett. Because they were living in sin – according to common belief – compassion for the dead girl was minimal. The year before, Hallett had been locked up for threatening to murder the young woman.

Four persons were present at the cottage on the night of the murder: Hallet, Mary Anne, Hallett's son, and the girl's father-in-law, Samuel Saunders. It was Saunders who recounted the events.

It was a horrible winter's night and the three adults were all drunk. Saunders was too indisposed to go home and agreed to stay the night, sharing the bed of Hallett's son. At about five o'clock in the morning, they awoke to shouts from Mary Anne, calling for help. It was still dark and they could not find any matches to light a candle. Saunders admitted that he was still 'boozy', which added to his confusion. By the time they found their way downstairs, Mary, dressed in her chemise and stays, was on the floor, her head nearly severed from her body. Hallet was raving, blaming the drink. The police and a doctor were sent for. There was nothing to be done for Mary, and Hallet was carted away on the charge of killing her.

On the day of the trial, Hallet's soon-to-be-orphaned son cried bitterly as he gave evidence. It took the jury only a few minutes to reach a verdict of wilful murder.

A Drunkard and a Bully

After a miserable life at the hands of her abusive husband, Jane Lacey, of the Old House Farm at St Helens, was badly beaten and died from her injuries. Living in the house with the pair was Susan Wildey, Jane's niece, who had long been witness to the unhappy life endured by her aunt. In February 1861, Henry Lacey had gone into town, and, while he was away, Pricilla Young, a neighbour, had called to help Mrs Lacey to bed. At the time she was very frail, suffering from an inflammation of the bowel, which may well have been a symptom of her unhappy state of mind. Lacey returned home drunk, and the following morning another neighbour, Mrs Corney, called. She was immediately confronted by Lacey, who said that his wife was dead and that she had fallen down the stairs. His next words were guaranteed to arouse suspicion: 'I am as innocent as you are, I have not done anything, I have not done it.' Mrs Corney went upstairs and found the victim with severe bruising to her face and body. Pricilla Young was summoned and swore that there had been no such injuries the evening before.

The doctor was sent for and ascertained that Jane had been dead for some hours. He asked to have a private word with Susan Wildey, the niece, but Lacey pushed her into the house and said that anything that passed between them should be said in front of him. The doctor departed and returned later to find Lacey struggling with the police. He gave his opinion that it would have been well nigh impossible for Mrs Lacey to reach the stairs, being in such a debilitated condition.

Taken to court, Lacey, who was suffering from *delirium tremens* (shaking frenzies), was sent to Winchester to stand trial. The jury convicted him of manslaughter and he was sentenced to six months in gaol.

Leonard Stone on the Slippery Slope

In early 1907, twenty-one-year-old Leonard Hugh Stone appeared in court for stealing a ferret. His petty crime barely deserves a mention, except for the fact that six weeks later he was charged with attempted murder.

Stone was born in Ryde, in 1863, and nothing has been recorded about his young life, but it is known that he made a living as a travelling hawker.

At some point he met eighteen-year-old Julie Ann Gatehouse, who came from Hove in Sussex. Whatever passed between them, one day he took her to Ashey Woods and tried to murder her – first by attempting to cut her throat and then by hanging her with a rope. Stone was declared insane and incarcerated in an asylum, but only until 4 October 1907. How he spent the next three years

The murder of Julie Ann Gatehouse.

is not known, but in 1910 he appeared in court in Aberdeen, charged with rape. The case was unproven but, having also carried out an assault, he received eighteen months' hard labour. Thereafter he disappears from history.

Murder Against Oneself

Until 1961, the act of suicide was a crime and attempted suicide was a prosecutable offence. The threat of damnation and confiscation of the family's assets meant that suicide was a terrible step, and where possible the facts were covered up by those left behind. The coroner regularly concluded that the reason for the death was 'a case of insanity', as evidenced by the various entries in his book. In 1852 the following cases were recorded:

21 January: Robert Bryant of Newport aged forty-nine, hanged himself while in a state of insanity.
23 January: David Horlock Jeffery of Yaverland, aged thirty-seven, 'died from the effects of immersion in the sea into which he had walked while in a state of insanity'.
11 September: Charles Small of Newport, aged twenty-three. 'The deceased hanged himself but no sufficient evidence to show his state of mind at the time.'

The Case of John Hooke

In 1667 the Court Book of Newport recorded that John Hooke, grocer of that town, had died at his own hand by hanging. The son of a clergyman at Freshwater, John appeared to have made his way into respectable Newport society, having become a burgess of the Borough, then treasurer for the Corporation and finally Mayor of Newport. These posts, however, came at a financial cost and it seems that in trying to keep up with the Jones', John had ended up in debt.

John was the eldest of two brothers. His sibling Robert, who had been born weak and sickly, was now in London achieving acclaim for his scientific work and publications. This may have added to John's growing sense of failure. Indeed, he had borrowed several hundred pounds from Robert and was still struggling to pay his way.

Having died at his own hand, thus committing a mortal sin, John was not buried in hallowed ground. Following the inquest, his goods and chattels were seized and a public sale was announced for a Saturday – market day in Newport. The money raised came to £60 19s 9d. Thereafter, anyone owed money by the dead man could present his bill.

The Corporation undertook to pay for Mrs Hooke's board and lodging and granted her £10 a year for her lifetime – a sorry ending for this pillar of society.

The Sorry Case of George Mundell

In August 1912, George Mundell, an elderly man, was up in court on a charge of stealing coal from Newport Railway Yard. There had been complaints about thefts and a constable was keeping watch when he saw George secrete a small amount of coal in his pockets. When approached, he begged not to be arrested, pleading to be spared because of his three small children at home, but the constable took him into custody nevertheless. However, as they crossed the bridge, George broke free, climbed onto the balustrade and threw himself 17ft into the water. Constable Stevens dived in to save him while Mundell said repeatedly, 'I wish I was dead.' He had not been in any trouble before.

George was tried jointly for theft and attempting suicide. An older son of his, who lived in Portsmouth, came forward to say that he was willing to take his father in if the court would release him. In his defence, George said it was poverty that drove him to steal and that this was the greatest disaster of his life.

He pleaded guilty to both charges but in view of the circumstances of the theft, the charge was dismissed. In the view of the medical officer, George needed to be looked after and it was agreed that he should go to his son. As the second case was dismissed, the court cheered.

Between January 1900 and June 1906, forty-seven verdicts of suicide were recorded by the Island coroner.

Burglary and Theft

Murder was only one of many crimes punishable by death. At the March Assizes in 1819, the *Salisbury and Winchester Journal* reported that sixteen prisoners were sentenced to execution, among whom were George Underwood, who robbed the house of George Ward at Northwood Park in Cowes, and Thomas Reynolds for robbing the house of William Hendicott at Thorley.

The *Journal* solemnly confirmed that the 'awful sentence of death' was passed on the men. Both had previous convictions.

Underwood and Reynalds en route to the scaffold.

At the same Assizes, Henry Handley was found guilty of slaying Edward Saunders at Arreton, but rather than being sentenced to death he was fined £100 and imprisoned for six months. Perhaps this was because it was his first offence, or maybe because he was a 'gentleman'.

Raggle Taggle Gypsies

On 21 March 1825, John Smith (real name Hughes), James Dawes and William Dawes were sentenced to death for horse stealing. Hughes described himself as a rat-catcher and basket-maker, but the *Salisbury and Winchester Journal* said that he made his living mainly by plunder in many counties. The Dawes brothers burgled a house at Binstead and left a letter implicating a third party. However, when arrested they confessed it was false. In sentencing them to death, the court announced that the chief cause of their downfall was 'Sabbath breaking and poaching'. Before they were despatched to meet their 'Redeemer', they were urged to repent and ask his forgiveness.

Not Learning One's Lesson?

The *Salisbury and Winchester Journal* of 9 July 1825 reported the arrest of Richard Rogers, for stealing a horse on the Island. When the case came to court in Winchester, he was acquitted because the owner of the horse failed to identify it. Having had one escape, however, Rogers was soon back in court again, this time for passing counterfeit money. When arrested, he had in his possession sovereigns, half crowns and shillings that were believed to be payment for a consignment of illegal liquor smuggled on to the Island. Rogers was known to travel frequently to the mainland for the purpose of distributing the contraband. His brother was also arrested. This time he was found guilty and sentenced to seven years' transportation.

On Saturday, 16 July 1825, David Dibden was accused of taking a gelding from William Taylor of Godshill. He was less fortunate than Rogers and sentenced to death. At the last minute, however, he was reprieved.

On 5 February 1825, Charles Crawley and George Chiverall were sentenced to death for burglary. They had robbed the house of Ann Shute at Whippingham.

Rustling!

Thomas Prior stole one game fowl belonging to John Blundell of the Isle of Wight and was sentenced to serve six months in prison.

Alexander White and Emily Webb both found themselves in court. White stole a turkey and a fowl from George Goodeve of Binstead, and Emily was accused of accepting them even though she knew they were stolen.

George Racket, Stephen Kimber and George Downden were each sentenced to seven years' transportation for stealing poultry and timber.

James White ended up in gaol for stealing three pigs at Brading, the property of Edward Bull.

James White, the piper's son?

What's for Supper?

In 1948 a local man, James, found himself in court following the theft of lead from Medina Mill. In his defence, he explained that his wife hadn't been well and said that she fancied a hedgehog, so he drove down to Stagg Lane Newport to look for one. On the way, his lorry hit something in the road and he discovered a piece of lead. He put it in the back of the lorry with no thought as to stealing it. Whether or not he found a hedgehog it doesn't say, but he was fined £2.

Drunk and Disorderly

When Revd Henry Worsley made a complaint against George Morris and John Brown for being drunk on a Sunday, it was Edward Morris who ended up in gaol, having refused to give evidence against the two revellers. He received seven days in the bridewell.

James Cassford of Ventnor held a dubious honour of being convicted of drunkenness more often than any living man. March 1861 found him in court for the same offence, and he was packed off to his familiar lodgings at Winchester Gaol to serve a month.

Rather smugly, on 21 October 1825, at Newport Quarter Sessions held in the Guildhall, the deputy recorder Mr Thomas Sewell congratulated the grand jury on the appearance of the calendar, which contained very few cases indeed. Joseph Cowdrey, a Newport grocer who assaulted William Salter, his brother's apprentice, was one of the few cases that came before the court. He was fined 40s. Rather more boisterously, George Burrows and others were convicted of causing a riot. Quite what happened, it does not say, but George received fourteen days' confinement to hard labour in the bridewell. John Hobbs of Yarmouth failed to keep up payments towards the cost of his bastard child and, having no surety, also found himself in the bridewell.

Bound Apprentice

An apprenticeship was a legal contract not to be broken lightly. In May 1786, the *Salisbury and Winchester Journal* carried the following warning:

> Benjamin Young an apprentice to a carpenter and joiner (at Newport) lately eloped from his master. He is twenty years old, about five feet five inches in height and rather thickset. This is to caution all persons not to employ or harbour the said apprentice, as they will be prosecuted for the same.

Failing to Pay Up

When Mr Lush took a post for a year's appointment as an usher at Mr May's academy at West Cowes, he was awarded the annual salary of £33. Having started his term at the end of the Christmas vacation, he completed his service at the beginning of the following Christmas period of 1819. Mr May then refused to pay, saying that Lush had not served for a full year. On taking the matter to court, the case was found for the plaintiff and the full amount awarded.

A Day's Pay

William Beck, captain of the ship *William IV*, was called to explain why he had failed to pay two day-workers, John Bannister and Charles Fellowes, the agreed sum of 3s 6d. Beck said that he had given them 2s and 7d, as in his view they had only worked for three-quarters of the agreed time, starting at 10 a.m. and stopping at 6 p.m. The plaintiffs replied that the hours for all water-men at the custom house were from 8 a.m. to 4 p.m., and in any case they had taken the work to be paid by the job, not the hour. The court found in their favour; Beck was instructed to pay the additional wages, plus 9s costs, and told to be clearer next time he entered into any such arrangement. (From the *Hampshire Telegraph*, 1861)

Riotous Behaviour

The first day of the Assizes at Newport, on 25 January 1826, saw John Wheeler, William Cushion, Henry Parker, James James and James Redstone all found guilty of riot and assault. They were each sentenced to 'three months in our bridewell'.

Newport Bridewell, named for one of Henry VIII's palaces, was situated at the bottom of Holyrood Street and Crocker Street, on land now occupied by sheltered housing.

Island Lads Gone Bad Abroad

Not all locally-born criminals remained on the Island. The national census of 1881 showed the following:

Held in Woking Prison
Robert Small, born 1830 at West Cowes: In July 1855 Small was accused of manslaughter but found not guilty. There then followed several convictions for larceny and in January 1869 he was sentenced to six months' gaol. In 1876 he was again charged with larceny when he was already under police supervision, and sentenced to nine years. It was following this

sentence that he found himself in the Woking Invalid Prison in 1881.

In 1891, the following cases were recorded in Dartmoor:

George Newbury was born in 1845 at Newbridge. October 1880 saw him charged with larceny at Winchester Crown Court. Having two previous convictions, he was sentenced to two years' imprisonment. In 1884, using the name James Taylor, he was again convicted of larceny at Winchester and given seven years. In 1892, again under the name of Taylor, he was accused of common assault and sentenced to four months. In 1891 he found himself again in Dartmoor for an un-named crime.

Ashford Young was born in 1837 at Brading. In March 1875 he was sentenced to three months' hard labour at Winchester for larceny. April 1878 saw him imprisoned for eight months for obtaining goods by false pretences, and in 1880 at Winchester there followed a ten month sentence with two years' supervision for larceny. By November 1881, they upped the anti and he was sentenced to five years for forgery. In June 1886 he received another five years for larceny followed in October 1891 by a six-year sentence for obtaining food and drink by false pretences. Between each term of imprisonment, he seems to have returned to the Island and then been sent to Winchester for the next trial. Finally, 1891 found him incarcerated in Dartmoor.

Sentenced to Death

During the eighteenth and nineteenth centuries, some Islanders found themselves on trial at the Old Bailey.

On Monday, 20 May 1717, Thomas Price, aged seventeen, was charged with burglary. Thomas was born at Carisbrooke and brought up at sea, suggesting that he was probably an orphan raised by the parish. He served latterly on the *Burford*, a man-of-war, having been recently discharged at Portsmouth. Coming to London to look for another ship, he took lodgings with Edward

Goodson, who was later to give evidence against him. He was condemned for stealing two silver cups, seven spoons, a watch and clothing from Dr Guy Mesmin, all valued at £40. He admitted to some of the charges, stating that he had been 'very wicked'.

Price was sentenced to be executed at Tyburn on 20 May. En route to the scaffold, he and others were accompanied by Paul Lorrain, the 'ordinary' or chaplain, who made them recite the Apostle's Creed and sing psalms.

Happier was the case of Richard Potter, aka Pollard, a twenty-year-old born on the Island and bred to the sea from the age of ten. His trial took place on 24 August 1763. He was involved first in the coasting trade and then sailed to Africa on board *St Janiero*, a Spanish prize. This man feloniously assumed the name and character of Andrew McGee in order to claim prize money due to him for his service on the *Burford*. After being arrested, he learned to read and because of his good behaviour was reprieved.

A Case of Deception

When John Potter died suddenly on 14 March 1783 in St Helena, his shipmate, James Dunn, saw a chance to earn some money. Claiming to be Potter's executor and also his cousin, he presented a will to the United Company of Merchants trading in the West Indies, swearing that he had witnessed the signing of the will and knew the other witnesses. An investigation was carried out and, unfortunately for Dunn, Potter's wife came forward and produced letters of administration. Dunn swore that both he and his dead cousin came from the Isle of Wight, but when questioned he was unaware that Dunn had a wife and children. He was found guilty of presenting a false, forged and counterfeited will and testament. The death sentence was the punishment dealt.

An 'Innocent' Abroad?

Before the court at the Old Bailey, on 16 October 1765, was John Majour of Newport, who found that the allure of the city flesh-pots were not all they were cracked up to be. He seems to have visited London before and enjoyed the experience, for he told the court that going to the Three Lemons for some refreshment, he enquired after a 'certain person', but was told that she had gone to Gravesend. No doubt disappointed, he then chose another young lady to drink a glass of wine with him, but as he got out his green purse to pay, she snatched it away and ran off with Majour in pursuit. She evaded him and he could do nothing but shout that he had been robbed. A constable was summoned and took up the pursuit. In the purse were 4 guineas, one half-guinea, one quarter-guinea, a moidore and some silver. There was also a confrontation in the Three Lemons, when the waiter accused Majour of not paying his bill.

Following this fiasco, a young woman, Jane Ponsonby, found herself in court accused of theft. In the course of the examination, Majour admitted that before meeting Jane in the Three Lemons, he had already had two or three pints of wine in Goodman's Fields and had been at another house at 10 a.m. , where he had drunk two pints of 'half and half'. Mention was also made of changing a guinea at the Fox.

Jane Ponsonby denied stealing his money. A witness, Grizzle Hussey, described how she had visited the landlady of the Three Lemons, a gentlewoman who was breastfeeding her child, when Majour came in and grabbed the accused by the arm, calling her 'you bitch of hell flames!' Hussey said that Majour was 'very much in liquor'.

As there was no clear evidence that Ms Ponsonby had stolen the purse, she was acquitted. Mr Majour, who previously served aboard a man-of-war, was a poorer and perhaps a wiser man.

Chapter Two

The Military: There's Something About a Soldier

The Tartan Army

In 1627 the Governor of the Isle of Wight, Sir John Conway, received the news that 1,000 men, under Colonel Brett, were to be billeted on Island shores. This immediately raised the question of where they would go and how they would be fed. Despite local protest, they arrived on 6 May and stayed until 21 June.

After the visit, the commentator on all things local, Sir John Oglander, recorded in his diary that things had worked out better than expected. The Islanders had been satisfied with the arrangement, having been well paid for the service. Oglander wrote that they wouldn't mind something similar happening in future. It was soon, however, a question of being careful what you wish for...

In November 1627, Governor Conway received news that a further 1,500 men were to be despatched to the Isle of Wight. Although the Island was only one eighth of the size of Hampshire, the number of troops arriving constituted a quarter of all those in the kingdom. With hindsight, this was bound to be a recipe for disaster.

While this news was being absorbed, a further communication reported that yet more soldiers were docking in the Solent and were likely to mutiny if they were not allowed ashore. Protest was useless. The said soldiers disembarked and remained until September 1628.

They turned out to be a regiment of Scottish soldiers, and according to Sir John they were unused to the niceties of society. Although 700 of their officers claimed to be 'gentlemen', Sir John was appalled at their table manners. Any willingness to house the visitors quickly evaporated. Bills for their keep were soon overdue and the men were wild and quarrelsome. Sir John said, 'They lay here a long time to the great sorrow, loss and undoing of the whole Island.' He further reported that they committed 'diverse murders, rapes, robberies, burglaries, getting of bastards and almost the undoing of the whole Island…'

Rather than increasing the safety of the Wight by their presence, Governor Conway wrote to the commanding officer of the regiment, the Earl of Morton, demanding that 'redress must bee had or the Island utterly spoyled [sic]'.

Special powers existed along with martial law, but Conway soon found, to his cost, that the visiting officers had little interest in preventing or punishing crime. On 16 June, men serving in Sir William Carr's company carried out a murder, and although the crime was quickly reported, no speedy action was taken by the military. In the end, Sir Robert Dillington, as the local commissioner, raised the hue and cry and scoured the area himself until three suspects were found in a local alehouse. He tried to question them but they refused to answer, and he found himself helpless.

It quickly became clear that the Scottish officers would offer no help. Meanwhile, the local authorities were intimidated and dared not take action. Sir Robert vented his frustration by arresting local Island men who had refused to take part in the hue and cry, no doubt from fear of reprisals.

On 4 August 1628, Sir John Oglander was part of a delegation who petitioned the King about these unwelcome allies. King Charles asked them to be patient, sent his thanks to the Islanders for their kindness to the Scots, treated the delegation to dinner and said he would inform the Duke of Buckingham, his effete and useless adviser. On 23 August, Buckingham was murdered.

By the time sufficient money was found to despatch the unwelcome intruders back to Scotland, they left behind a string of offences. The State Papers recorded a murder of a man named Stevens at Brixton, by a soldier of Sir George Hayes' Company; a burglary at Newport by one of Earl of Morton's Company; and a rape at Northwood carried out by *a* Highlander, one of Captain Maknaughton's Company. In addition, the Scots carried out a series of highway robberies, damaged timber and poached 'his Majestie's deare both in the parke and forrest [*sic*]'.

The soldiers finally departed amid a collected sigh of relief. Sir John declared that he never wished to see a 'Scotchman' again. Looking on the bright side, though, he was further thankful that they had not been lumbered with Englishmen returning from the Continent, who would no doubt have brought 'the infectious disease wherewith they corrupted all places where they came'. Sir John was undoubtedly an optimist.

In 1631, £3,000 was finally paid towards the cost of the billeting. The actual sum due was £7,340. By 1635 there was no evidence that the remainder had been paid.

Don't Panic!

The Scottish experience aside, Islanders were often looking over their shoulders expecting attack. Sir John Oglander's *Royalist's Notebook*, 1622–1652, reported a rumour of an imminent invasion at St Helens on 24 May 1624. Sir John immediately went to investigate. En route he received further reports that 500 Hamburgers had landed, the number quickly increasing to 1,000. In the event, the alert was soon over – as this turned out to be a false alarm – but to Sir John's chagrin, his servant, Mr Way, had lit the beacon without permission. So annoyed was Sir John that he sent the poor man to the castle prison.

Move Over Captain Mainwaring

Right up until the mid-twentieth century, a military presence was the norm, and at the time of the D-Day landings, it was claimed that the Isle of Wight was so crowded with soldiers that it would have been impossible to land even one more.

Some idea of the numbers and location of troops on the Island may be inferred from the records of Sacrament Certificates issued to officers across the Island. These certificates marked the taking of Holy Communion and were associated with the oaths of loyalty taken by persons of authority, both to the King and to the Church of England. In July 1673, the following certificates were issued:

> To Captain James Haskall's Company in Newport: eight certificates. James Halsall himself received a certificate as Deputy Governor of the Isle of Wight.

> To the Company of Militia Foot in Newport, under the Command of Captain Nicholas Chestle: five certificates

> To the Company of Militia Foot under the Command of Major William Stephens: five certificates

In the same month the following officers also received their certificates:

> Anthony Dove, ensign of the Company of Militia Foot, under the command of Major Thomas Knight in the regiment of the East Medine

Robert How the elder, gunner of His Majesty's Castle, Carisbrooke

Robert How the younger, drummer

By 1689, the number of troops serving on the Island had risen dramatically – as shown by the number of certificates issued to officers in June and July of that year:

Troop of horse under the command of the Honourable Colonel Charles Godfrey: nine certificates

The Honourable Colonel Francis Lutterell's Company of Foot: twenty-six certificates

We're Doomed!

It would have been a miracle if these numerous troops – mainly unwilling volunteers, bored and a long way from home – had not got into mischief.

John Sargent from Wool Lavington in Sussex, visiting his son-in-law, Revd Samuel Wilberforce (later one of the three bishops after whom the pub at Brighstone is named), described the village as 'notorious for villainy and loose living due to the influence of the barracks and smugglers'. Disputes between the locals and the military were not uncommon.

The Demon Drink

Many problems arising from the army presence involved alcohol. The habit of billeting soldiers in pubs almost certainly added to the problem.

At Winchester Assizes on 9 March 1812, two soldiers from the Island were in court for breaking into the Tontine Inn at Newport, where one of them, Andrew Ferguson, was billeted. In evidence, another soldier, Thomas Crompton, said that along with

Ferguson and Thomas Cassidy, who was billeted at the Fountain Inn, he had been drinking at the Tontine. Ferguson told him he had removed the pin from the shutters of the window and that he and Cassidy intended to rob the house, inviting Crompton to join them. Cassidy declared that he had seen Mrs Tharle, wife of the landlord, place a note in a drawer, where there were apparently fifty more; they planned to steal them. Cassidy further advocated blacking their faces and murdering the innkeeper and his wife, to which Crompton replied, 'For God's sake, do no murder.'

However, he went along with the burglary, and at the premises a quantity of copper, a pair of shoes and other items were stolen. The following morning, now sober, Crompton confessed to his sergeant and Ferguson and Cassidy were arrested. In their defence, they said that they had been drinking in the company of other soldiers and it must have been them who carried out the robbery, as they were innocent. They were found guilty and sentenced to death.

The soldiers were often resented by local inhabitants. As Private James Waldron was walking up Ryde High Street on 21 November 1822, he was jostled by a local man, John Denham. Having pushed him, Denham called him names and then struck him across the neck. The resulting fracas attracted the attention of several locals, who restrained Denham while Waldron and his companion, a corporal, escaped to their billet in the Black Horse Inn. At the time, Waldron had been sent to Ryde to assist the Ryde Customs. The incident was reported to the Inspecting Commander of the Customs and Denham was arrested. By the time the case came to court in late December, the corporal had been posted to the West Indies, and although Waldron should have left for Scotland, he was retained on the Island to give evidence. As there were several witnesses, Denham did not deny the charge and was very apologetic, offering to compensate Waldron for his injuries. In the event, the jury fined him £3. A payment was also made to Waldron for the expense he had incurred by remaining in the town

Another alcohol-related incident ended in death in September 1827, when soldiers of the 87th Regiment at Albany Barracks received their arrears of pay. That evening a number of men were returning to the barracks 'having drunk freely', when one of their number jumped aboard a passing dray and sat astride a tub. Unfortunately, he lost his balance and fell to the ground; the wheel of the dray passed over his chest. He was taken to hospital but 'his life [was] despaired of '.

In August 1860, the *Hampshire Telegraph* reported how William Meads, Patrick Mooney, Henry Kelly and James Carey – four privates in the Royal Artillery – had assaulted James Blandford, the landlord of the King's Head at Yarmouth. The four were remanded in custody.

On 2 February 1861 the *Hampshire Telegraph* carried a report that William Mather, a private in the 50th Regiment and a member of a party working on a well at the barracks, lost his balance and fell to his death down the well shaft. The verdict recorded that Mather was 'accidentally killed by attempting to descend a well in a state of intoxication'.

Alcohol was often to blame for unfortunate incidents in the army.

The Fairlee Flasher

August 1860 saw Jacob Gridley, a private in the 96th Regiment, accused by local girls Rosanna Holley and Mary Ann Wickens of exposing himself to them on the highway along Fairlee Road. Gridley had twice been in trouble for the same offence and had served three months in prison. The court had no hesitation in sentencing him to a further three months in Winchester Gaol.

It wasn't only the serving soldiers who got into trouble. In 1816, Alexander Davison Esq of St James' Square London, formerly Treasurer of the Ordinance, had the contract for supplying coal to the troops in the Isle of Wight cancelled. He was accused of falsely accounting and, following a trial, was locked up in Newgate Gaol.

Private Gridley reveals his secret weapon.

Albany Barracks

When the Napoleonic Wars were at their peak, a permanent military base was established at Parkhurst, just north of Newport, known as Albany Barracks.

The barracks were described by nineteenth-century writer Thomas Brettell as 'occupying a piece of ground 1,211ft by 700ft with five officers' houses, eight large and twelve small barracks, with outhouses attached and an excellent house for the Commandant and another for the Chief Accountant. The chapel is on the south side of the parade plus other buildings. Water comes from three excellent wells about 285ft deep and operated by engine pumps. The parade ground is second only to that at Chatham.'

The building work commenced in September 1798 and the site was named for the late Duke of York and Albany.

The hospital erected north of the barracks had four large and sixteen small wards, with iron bedsteads. The surgeon's house was in the centre and the stores to the rear. It covered 2 acres of ground. A piece of walled ground 100 square yards was the burial ground, facing the Cowes Road. The total area of barracks and hospital comprised 100 acres, encircled by a good plantation.

Albany Barracks opened its doors as the aftermath of the French Revolution threatened Britain. The site housed 2,040 men. Following their arrival, a word of warning was issued locally: 'Much as their military uniforms tend to enliven the dullness of a country town, the moral effects of such a congregation of the young and thoughtless, on the people of Newport, are very undesirable.'

A Duel to the Death

In 1813 a duel was fought at Carisbrooke Castle. Two lieutenants, based at Parkhurst Barracks, had fallen out. Some weeks earlier, John Blundell had married, asking his friend Edward McGuire to give the bride away, which he did. A little later, Blundell told several people that he had leant McGuire clothes to wear at the ceremony; McGuire took offence to this. At the time, the men were camped at Niton and their squabble, at the White Lion pub, turned nasty. Egged on by their companions, neither man could see a way out without losing face, so on Friday 9 July they went to Carisbrooke and duly fired two shots at each other. McGuire's second shot fatally wounded Blundell, who died three days later. McGuire and his companions were tried for murder, found guilty

A duel to the death.

and sentenced to death. Happily, at the behest of the Prince of Wales, they were pardoned.

In December 1813, a fatal duel took place in Northwood Park. The deceased was Lieutenant Cochrane Sutton, who planned to leave the following day on the vessel *Grace,* bound for South America. Passing time in the Dolphin Inn at Cowes, he was in the company of Major Orlando Lockyer, Thomas Redesdale and a Lieutenant Robert Hand. The *Grace* had been seized by customs at Cowes for various discrepancies, and because of the delay the passengers were all kicking their heels. When a fellow officer was called from the room, Sutton made a casual observation: 'We are a parcel of damned idle fellows and are leaving the country to get away from our creditors.' His remark upset Lockyer, who immediately accused him of calling him a debtor. Sutton added that they were all in the debt of God, but Lockyear was not appeased. Along with Redesdale and Hand they met the following morning at Northwood Park, where Lockyer fired a single shot, hitting Sutton in the heart. The three remaining men promptly vanished but were later arrested and appeared in court at Winchester. In his defence, Lockyear said that even on the way to the duel he had tried to settle the matter amicably with Sutton, but he would not retract his statement. Whatever the truth of the matter, in view of Lockyear's military record, the charge was changed to manslaughter and the participants each received three month sentences in prison.

Major Lockyear did not enjoy the enforced proximity of his fellow criminals in gaol and, shortly after sentence, petitioned the court that his situation should be ameliorated on grounds of his deteriorating health. The two magistrates did not agree and were adverse to any relaxation in his favour.

At the same Assizes, William Johnson was found guilty of robbing Richard Trueman on the highway in the parish of Whippingham. He was sentenced to death, but it was reprieved before the punishment was carried out.

Cases at the Quarter Sessions

Inevitably there were dealings between military personnel and the locals. As a result, both soldiers and Islanders sometimes found themselves in court.

10 September 1796
Benjamin Linnington, labourer of Newport, was accused of assisting in the desertion of Daniel McCarty, a private in the 43rd Regiment of Foot. Fined £5.
On the same day, Daniel McCarty was fined £5 for receiving cloathes [sic] and other regimental necessaries from Linnington.

6 June 1807
Ann Hennen was charged with receiving and detaining a shirt from Richard Hand, a private in the 56th Regiment of Foot. Fined £5.

2 March 1813
Henry Morey, labourer of Newport assisted and harboured John King and William Battel, privates in the 1st Battalion of the Royals, and John Parker a private in the Hon. East India Company, deserters. The prosecutor was William Linnington. Fined £20.

19 April 1795
George Ross was accused of assaulting Edward Reynolds,

keeper of the House of Correction, in order to enable Michael
Sweatman Coffield, an officer in HM's 107th Regiment of
Foot, to escape.

28 October 1799
Several officers of HM Regiment of Birmingham Fencibles
were accused of assaulting Edward Bellingham Kennah, lieutenant in the regiment. Bellingham later went to fight in India
as paymaster to HM 25th Light Dragoons. He died at the age
of twenty-nine at Bangalore, where a monument is erected in
his honour.

Co-operation with the Revenue Men

In 1816, the customs and excise were so over-stretched that
Captain Mainwaring, Commandant of the Isle of Wight, reported
that he was forced to rely on the military for support. All public
houses situated near smuggling resorts called frequently, even
daily, for assistance. In his view, the distribution of the soldiers
at the inns was sufficient, and this was the best solution he could
think of. The only thing wanted was a little more urgency on the
part of the soldiers.

Court of Requests: Debts against the
Military

The Court of Requests dealt with minor cases of unpaid debt,
and the military sometimes came to its attention: Elizabeth
Hawkins successfully brought a case against Dr Powers, based at
the army depot, who owed her 8s 6d; George Hanson sued one V.
Wallery at the signal station for £1 10s and the case found for the
plaintiff; John Morgan of Albany Barracks owed John Gough for
lodgings and board, and when challenged he paid up; Lieutenant
Whalley at the signal house owed Doctor Watermouth 10s 1d
and also paid up; in November 1816 Willliam Farley of Parkhurst
owed Matthew Jones 11s 7d.

The Case of Three Australians, Eight Boers and a German Missionary

An international scandal saw Australian George Ramsdale Witton temporarily imprisoned on the Isle of Wight. Witton was a serving lieutenant in the Bushweldt Carbineers, fighting under the orders of Lord Kitchener during the Boer War in South Africa.

Following a raid on a farmhouse in the Transvaal, two officers in the Carbineers were killed. According to later testaments, one of the dead men, Captain Hunt, had been stamped on, slashed with knives and stripped of his uniform. After a successful counter attack, eight Boers, generally regarded as prisoners, were executed on the orders of Captains Harry Morant and Peter Handcock. A German missionary, who had seemed to be conspiring with them, was also shot.

Accused of illegally killing prisoners of war, Morant, Handcock and Witton, with four others, were put on trial. The two captains confirmed that when they found a Boer wearing Captain Hunt's uniform, they summarily executed him. They were acting on orders issued by General Kitchener himself – to take no prisoners. In his defence, Witton said that he had no reason to question the orders given to him by Captain Handcock that no prisoners were to be taken.

Even as the trial was in progress, an attack by Boers on the courthouse interrupted the proceedings and the prisoners joined in to fight off the onslaught, driving the enemy away. Their courageous actions made no difference to the outcome of their trial and the court found all three men guilty of murdering the Boers, but not the missionary. They recommended mercy.

The plea was ignored and Lord Kitchener himself signed the death sentence for Morant and Handcock, but he commuted Witton's sentence to life imprisonment.

Morant and Handcock were executed by firing squad at Pretoria Gaol. Handcock's wife later read about her husband's fate in a newspaper. Witton was shipped to England to serve his sentence, originally being incarcerated on the Island but later transferred to Portland. The case caused controversy and three years later his sentence was overturned by the House of Commons.

On gaining his freedom, Witton wrote an account of the events in South Africa entitled 'Scapegoats of the Empire: The True Story of Breaker Morant's Bushweldt Carbineers'. The story was later turned into a film.

George Witton returned home to Queensland, married, and ran a dairy farm producing cheese. The stigma of events in the Transvaal remained with him.

General Kitchener later admitted that he had given orders that any Boer found wearing a British uniform was to be shot.

A Crime of the Most Revolting Nature

On 10 December 1810, forty-two-year-old ensign John Newbolt Hepburn, of the 4th West India Regiment, was apprehended at Newport Barracks. Along with sixteen-year-old T. White, a drummer boy, he was accused of a detestable crime, which had taken place at the Vere Street Club in London.

The pair appeared at the Old Bailey and were duly found guilty. On 8 March 1811, before eight o'clock in the morning, they were both taken to the scaffold erected outside the debtors' door at the Old Bailey; there they were executed. Among those gathering to enjoy the event were the Duke of Cumberland, Lord Sefton and Lord Yarmouth. On the same day, poor White's mother died, her death attributed to a broken heart.

Suicide

A verdict on Michael Connel, aged twenty-one, at Parkhurst Barracks, concluded that he shot himself but there was not enough evidence to decide if he was of unsound mind. The cost of the enquiry amounted to £2 7s 5d.

In 1911, questions were asked in Parliament about the suicides of three soldiers in Parkhurst Military Hospital – concerns were voiced as to whether the hospital staff were overworked.

Soldiers' Revolt

According to the *Isle of Wight Observer* in 1861, when John Thomas Gells was accused of deserting from the Hants Militia Infantry he denied ever having been in the army and declared himself to be unfit for military service.

In February 1876, the same newspaper reported that Sergeant Heal of the Isle of Wight Artillery Militia was allowed £1 for having apprehended George Dyer, a deserter. Dyer was sent to Winchester to await the action of the War Office.

In December 1903, about fifty men of the Sherwood Foresters, based at Parkhurst, had to be rounded up by both police and locals when their farewell celebrations got out of hand. The men were shortly leaving for Hong Kong and about 200 soldiers in total went into Newport for a night out. As the evening passed, the initial noise and rowdiness degenerated into drunken brawls. In the Holyrood Street area, thirty windows were shattered. The fried fish shop in the High Street was invaded and the battered cod taken, the owner succumbing rather than risk further damage.

'We've had our chips!'

A combination of soldiers, local men and merry-making women reached gathered in Lower St James' Street, where the military – somewhat the worse for wear – wove their way back towards the barracks. The military police arrived but were unable to quell the chaos, and a combined effort by the local constabulary, the military police and local citizens was needed to herd the soldiers back towards their barracks. The regiment had to pay for all the damage caused.

Summarily Dealt With

The army invariably took care of its own, and in 1794 two Roman Catholic soldiers convicted of burglary were taken into Parkhurst Forest and hanged. Patrick Quire and Patrick Corne of the Prince of Wales' Irish Foot had broken into the house of Benjamin Calcott at Northwood and assaulted him and his wife.

Accordingly, at 3 a.m. they were taken from their cells and marched into the forest, where the execution was to take place at midday. The newspaper reported that the spectacle was watched by the biggest crowd ever to gather on the Isle of Wight. Even stranger, a mother with a sick child requested that one of the dead men's hands be placed on her child's neck, in the hope of its curative powers against the King's Evil. This was the first such execution to take place in sixty years.

Chapter Three

Spies and Insurrections

For a sleepy backwater, the Isle of Wight – guarding, as it does, the underbelly of England – was never far from the minds of politicians.

Which Queen Shall We Have?

In 1556, Richard Uvedale was appointed as Captain of Yarmouth Castle. Uvedale was born in about 1508, the son of William Uvedale, a landowner of some standing in Hampshire. His parents had eight children and William was the fourth son. His father died when he was twenty and his mother went on to remarry, becoming stepmother to King Henry VIII's future Queen, Katherine Howard.

As a young man, Richard went to France. On his return, a family acquaintance, Sir Richard Long – a member of the Privy Council – arranged for his appointment as Captain of Hasilworth Castle, which stood near the entry to Portsmouth Harbour. Then, in about 1552, he was transferred as the first Captain of Yarmouth Castle.

At this time, his life was one round of socialising and hunting. After his appointment to Yarmouth, however, his cosy existence was thrown into chaos when he became acquainted with Sir Henry Dudley.

Dudley had already been associated with plans to oust Queen Mary I from the throne and replace her with Lady Jane Gray. This plan failed, but the marriage of Queen Mary to Phillip II of Spain caused widespread discontent, exacerbated by the suggestion that Phillip would be crowned King of England.

Dudley, who made frequent voyages to France in his role as a Vice Admiral, was in a position to co-ordinate opposition to the marriage on both sides of the Channel. Enthusiastic, persuasive and prone to exaggeration, he convinced many people, including Uvedale, of the viability of replacing the Queen by her sister Elizabeth. In this, he was supported by John Throckmorton, a Gloucester man who was also known to Uvedale. Thus, Yarmouth's Captain was persuaded to prepare Yarmouth Harbour and Castle to receive foreign help from France. It was his job to rally the troops locally; the combined force would march from the Isle of Wight to London.

Uvedale agreed to make several unlicensed trips across the Channel, taking Dudley with him. Inevitably word of the plot reached the English court. Uvedale was arrested and at first denied all knowledge of the plot, although he admitted transporting Dudley to France, insisting that as far as he was aware, Dudley was leaving the country to avoid his debts. He claimed that on the voyage, Dudley and Throckmorton had communicated in French, a language he did not understand, and wrote letters in code that he did not see.

Uvedale was removed to London, and under 'intense interrogation' provided the government with the information they sought – in the process also condemning himself. Other conspirators, likewise, cracked under pressure and a fellow plotter, John Bedell, stated that he had witnessed Uvedale promising to sabotage the English fleet.

Uvedale had been regarded as an essential part of the plot, as he had access to the Island gentry, and Dudley had been able to assure the French that he could easily raise a local force of up to 2,000. The actual garrison at Yarmouth consisted of one master gunner, one porter and seventeen soldiers.

Uvedale, a bachelor, was tried and found guilty at Southwark on 21 April 1556. A week later he was executed at Tyburn. John

Pearse, shipmaster of Southampton, reported that on the 'twenty-eighth day of April was draune from the Towre at Tyborne 2 gentyllmen, on ys name was Master Waddall [Uvdale] captayn of the Yle of Wyth and the odur wase master John Frogmorton and so hangyed and after cut down and quartered, and the morrow after there hedes set on London Bryge [sic].'

Throckmorton met a similar fate but Dudley was conveniently installed in France, where he stayed until Queen Elizabeth ascended to the throne.

Sir William Girling

While Uvedale and Throckmorton, along with six others, met a grisly end following the Dudley Conspiracy, Sir William Girling – Queen Mary's choice as Captain of the Isle of Wight – also ended up in trouble. Girling probably came from a Suffolk family and was described as 'a man of low extraction', having no coat of arms. His appointment was not welcome and he was soon accused of failing to keep the Island's defences ready against attack. The monies allocated for this task seems to have gone into his pocket. Like Uvedale he was named as one of the conspirators planning to oust the Queen, but he did not meet their fate. His role as Captain lasted from 1554–6 and what became of him is uncertain, although there is a suggestion that in 1588, as the Armada threatened the Island, he was called back into service. His public performance, however, was not a glorious affair.

Louis de Rochefort

The former Waxworks building at Brading is known as the oldest house on the Island. Originally it was the rectory, and it dates from at least 1228. During its existence it has had various incarnations.

In the sixteenth/seventeenth century, the building was the Crown Inn and here, in the 1640s, Louis de Rochefort – a French spy – came to deliver information to King Charles I. It would seem that parliamentary supporters noticed his presence, for

The skeleton was identified as being French.

Rochefort was assaulted. He died from his injuries and was hurriedly buried.

In 1960, while workmen were putting in a water main, they discovered his skeleton. It was identified and shipped across the Channel, but, finding no relatives in France, it was returned to Brading and put on display as part of the exhibition at the Old Waxworks. When the business closed in October 2009, the contents were auctioned off and, sadly, Louis seems to have left his resting place after more than 300 years.

The Great Escape

One of the most notorious spies of the eighteenth century was David Tyree, condemned to death in 1782 for conducting treasonable correspondence with the French.

A fellow prisoner in Winchester Gaol was Captain Maynard, formerly the landlord of the Vine Inn at West Cowes, who found himself behind bars for debt. With Tyree and others, he became involved in a plan to tunnel out of Winchester Gaol and, in return for being the look-out, Tyree promised to pay Maynard's debts.

The plans were far advanced and Maynard acquired a wig and a pair of 'trowsers' for Tyree to affect his escape. All may have been well if a fellow conspirator on the outside, who was instructed to buy tools from a village some distance away, had paid attention. Instead, he purchased them locally, thus arousing suspicion.

The plan was to set fire to the prison and abscond in the ensuing mayhem, but the plot was uncovered. Later, it was revealed that had the fire been started, twenty debtors locked in the room above would have met a certain death.

Tyree was moved to the condemned cell and Maynard, having aided the escape plan, was dealt seven years' transportation. Hoping to salvage something from the situation, Maynard swore that given access to Tyree, he would be able to exact important information from him, but his motives were suspected.

Tyree was removed to Portsmouth, where his grisly punishment took place. Here he was hanged, drawn and quartered; an estimated 100,000 people crowded to witness the spectacle.

The Most Dangerous Nazi Spy?

In August 1950, the Island woke up to the news that Dorothy Pamela O'Grady had returned to her Sandown home. It was ten years since she left, and most people did not believe that she would ever return to the modest boarding house she ran in the Broadway before the war.

Immediately, the debate started; was she or wasn't she guilty? Had she or hadn't she carried out the crimes for which she had been sentenced? Dorothy was now aged fifty-two and her last address had been Aylesbury Gaol, where she finished a nine-year stretch for spying.

Before the war, Dorothy had come to the Island with her husband, who was newly retired from the fire service. He was much older than his wife, being in his late sixties. When the Blitz threatened London, he responded to the call and went back to help, leaving Dorothy alone – except for her black retriever dog, Bob.

Back on the Island, things began to change. In a state of high alert, the beaches were barricaded to prevent the enemy from landing. Passes were needed to come to and from the Island, and blackouts were enforced rigorously, inspected by the ARP. In seemingly blissful ignorance, Dorothy and Bob proceeded to the beach and walked along the forbidden sands. Several times she was intercepted, and her excuse was that Bob needed his swim, as it was a hot summer. Her walks frequently took her towards Culver Cliff, above which stood Bembridge Fort – at that time a command post for anti-aircraft regiments, and also the HQ for the Home Guard. On one occasion, she was caught flashing a torch, defying blackout regulations. The authorities were thrown by the fact that she pinned a paper swastika to her coat and said how much she admired Hitler. They came to the conclusion that she was insane. She went too far, however, when she was discovered in the act of cutting telephone wires. She was arrested and found to be carrying various maps with areas marked on them.

Amazingly, although she was accused of crimes under the Treachery Act and of defying Defence Regulations, she was not held in custody. Instead she was summoned to appear before the Bench at Ryde. Not so amazingly, on the appointed day, Dorothy did not appear and she was eventually arrested at Yarmouth. Her excuse was that she had run away out of fear.

Dorothy was tried at the Hampshire Assizes, and because of the seriousness of the case, the trial was held in camera. Nine charges were brought against her and she was found guilty of seven of them. The judge, Mr Justice Macnaghton, announced, with due solemnity, that in the circumstances there was only one punishment that was permitted. He doffed a black cap and ordered that Dorothy should be hanged.

Her lawyers launched an appeal and, fortunately for Dorothy, two of the most serious charges were dropped. Her sentence was then changed to fourteen years in gaol. She was transferred to Holloway to serve her time.

The story now moves forward nine years, at which time Dorothy was released from gaol for good behaviour. Probably for monetary gain, she gave an interview to the *Daily Express*, explaining how the whole thing had been a foolish joke. Her oth-

A dangerous Nazi agent?

erwise uneventful life had been brightened by fantasies of what it would be like to be a spy. She even admitted that, as a young girl, she had written notes confessing to murdering her mother, but that none of them had been found. In fact, she had been fond of her mother and the notes were false.

As far as being a spy was concerned, rather clumsily she had laid a trail for the police, with the swastika on her coat and the maps in her bag on which she had marked various places. The actual moment of her sentence had been a thrill, but when she discovered that she was to be hanged rather than shot, she was disillusioned; she had imagined the drama of a firing squad.

During her time in gaol, Dorothy had found her niche as a maternal figure for many distraught young women. On her release, she turned her house into several bedsits to make some money. By 1971, she was becoming frail and was given accommodation in a warden-assisted flat at Porter Court in Lake. Here she remained for sixteen years until her death.

However, this is not the end of the story. In 2006, the records relating to Dorothy's case were released. Several journalists and the Island's MP took the opportunity to study them but, within weeks, the papers were recalled in connection with some 'official business'. Mysteriously, they were then mislaid and have not been returned to the public domain. At the time of Dorothy's trial, her defence lawyer's documents had been destroyed in an air attack, so the government files were of particular importance.

Dorothy had already admitted that she had been foolish and must have been suffering from some kind of mental 'kink'. Therefore, what the journalists concluded after seeing the papers is very revealing. The reporter from *The Times* wrote that the secret documents revealed she was 'not innocent... but a dangerous Nazi agent'. In the *Express* she was called 'the supreme mistress of the double bluff'. More emphatically, the *Mail* announced, 'Not only was she indeed a Nazi spy, she was one of the most dangerous and cunning they had ever recruited.'

Dorothy died in October 1985. The people who cared for her at the flat described her as nice, polite and appreciative of what was done for her. Not surprisingly, she did not talk about her war experiences or her time in gaol.

So who was Dorothy O'Grady? Was she a rather daft, foolish old lady, or a smart, ruthless enemy agent? Whichever the answer, she had the kudos of being the only woman sentenced to death for spying during the Second World War. Unless the government papers turn up, we will probably never know the truth.

Buses have Ears

In 1942, Doris Hannaford of Freshwater, who worked in a canteen at Cowes during the war, fell foul of the Defence of the Realm provisions. On 25 July, while on a bus, she was heard discussing shipping movements, and it was decreed that the information might 'directly or indirectly be of use to the enemy'. She was tried for a 'very serious offence' that could have been construed as treason. In the event, she was fined £10 and allowed two months in which to pay.

'So I said to Admiral Doenitz…'

Bonfires, Breakers and Captain Swing

Although separated from the mainland, the Island was not immune to the privations and agricultural unrest that affected the rest of the country.

The 1820s saw increasing discontent among the vast population of agricultural labourers. Several severe winters and poor harvests, plus long hours of toil and low wages, culminated in open mutiny in 1830. The last straw was the introduction of mechanical thresh-ing machines, depriving already desperate men of work. Across southern England, workers banded together and threatened their masters with arson, and worse if they failed to bring them relief.

A seemingly mythical leader, 'Captain Swing', emerged, a symbol of the men's struggle. Letters to targeted farmers and posters calling for action were signed in his name.

The machine breakers.

On 2 December 1830, Fanny Oglander, daughter of the well-established Nunwell family, wrote to her uncle, Colonel Henry Oglander, then serving in India. She told him of the latest disturbance. Hayricks at Newport and Freshwater, worth £200, had been burned, with further attempts at arson near Admiral's Lock at Gatehouse Farm, belonging to Mr Woodrow the butcher.

Two Island employers, Mr Woodrow and Mr Yelf, had purchased threshing machines and then received threatening letters from 'Swing', saying that everything they owned would be destroyed by fire. Mr Yelf abandoned the machine, so Mr Woodrow took it to his farm.

Mr Player of Ryde and Lady Holmes had also been threatened and special constables had been appointed at Newport and Ryde.

Fanny's brother William took up the story, writing to their uncle on 26 December, recounting the further disturbances among local labourers. As a result, some men had been transported for life while others got fourteen years. The severity of the sentences caused widespread dismay and many magistrates were sympathetic to their plight. Eventually, most were acquitted but the working conditions did not improve. 'Swing', of course, was never identified – probably because he didn't exist!

A Slice of the Cake?

In 1848, an upsurge of Chartism threatened to envelop the country, and Queen Victoria and her family were advised to retreat to Osborne House for their own safety. By June, their worst fears were confirmed when news arrived that a group was gathering at Cowes. Expecting murder at the very least, the military were summoned and navy personal aboard the royal ships at Cowes hastened to their Queen's defence. As the household staff stood by with rakes and broomsticks, the all clear was sounded. The insurgents at Cowes turned out to be a group of Oddfellows enjoying a day out.

'Fear not Your Majesty! We'll defend you.'

Walls Have Mouths

When Wilfred Macartney's book *Walls Have Mouths* was published in 1936, it spurred the Earl of Kinnoul to raise questions about prison conditions in the House of Lords.

Macartney's life is the stuff of the best spy stories. He was born in 1899 in Malta, and at the age of seventeen, inherited his father's valuable engineering enterprise, with a modern-day value of two million pounds.

Suave, well spoken and sporting a monocle, Macartney joined the army during the First World War. He found his way into military intelligence, operating in the Aegean. By the nature of such work, facts are always difficult to determine, but when the war ended, he seems to have continued his role in Ireland, working for British Intelligence with the Black and Tans.

Things began to unravel in the 1920s, and in February of 1926 he was sentenced to nine months' imprisonment for smashing a jeweller's window in London. After his release, he offered to sell his story as a spy with MI5, in defiance of the Official Secrets Act, then in 1926 he apparently joined the Communist Party.

Following a report that he was asking contacts for details of shipments to Finland, a trap was set and an obsolete naval manual was given to him. A raid was then made on the Soviet Trade Delegation, with the expectation of discovering it but, instead, they came upon a party of employees destroying secret papers. The manual was not among them, although it might have already been burned. There were, however, other suspect papers and on the strength of this, Macartney was arrested. He was charged under the Official Secrets Act and sentenced to ten years in gaol plus two years' hard labour. Much of his sentence was spent at Parkhurst.

Unsurprisingly, Macartney was well versed in the laws covering prisons. He was allotted to the tailor's shop, and when he was told to work on a straight jacket he refused to do so, stating that prisoners had the right not to work on articles of restraint.

Macartney described Parkhurst as 'a beastly prison... The cells were very damp and regarding the strong cells, there was no heating or windows. Men were often held there wearing only shirts and with only a blanket to lie on.' He claimed that at weekends,

Wilfred Macartney
– not as clever as
he thinks.

prisoners spent up to twenty-three hours in their cells, and men were reduced to smashing up cells and tearing up their clothes out of despair.

When the Earl of Kinnoull asked his questions in Parliament, they were largely dismissed – although it was admitted that, up until 1934, there was no electric light in the prison because there was not enough money to install it. Likewise, in 1937 there was still no running water.

After Macartney was released in December 1936, he left the country to join the Republicans in the Spanish Civil War. During the Second World War he worked under cover feeding false information to Hitler's regime.

When the war ended, he sold an account of his experiences to the French paper *Etoile de Soir* and was immediately arrested under the Official Secrets Act. He eventually made his way to Moscow where he died in 1953.

According to MI6, Marcartney was completely unscrupulous: 'He can never tell the truth about any matter, is very clever but not as clever as he thinks.'

I Spy

In the longstanding squabbles between the French and the English, the authorities were always on the lookout for spies. In 1789, as revolution flared in France, they arrested the artist George Morland at a house in Yarmouth.

Morland was on the run from his creditors, and to keep one step ahead had moved from one refuge to another around the Island. At Yarmouth some drawings were seized, reputed to be plans for a French invasion. He was frog marched into Newport, but witnesses came forward as to his 'good' character and the magistrates released him. During his stay on the Island, he produced many paintings of coastal scenes, smuggling and wrecking.

Morland visited the Island again in April 1799, staying with his wife at Cowes. Once again, he was pursued by debtors and only remained until November. In spite of his precarious financial position, he spent his time socialising with fishermen in local taverns, paying his way by dashing off a painting for the price of a drink. Having produced up to 4,000 art works, he died in 1804 at the age of forty-one.

The Curious Case of Captain Burley

Islander Captain John Burley was a devout Royalist, serving King Charles I throughout the Civil War. A one-time captain aboard the ship *Antelope*, he was dismissed when the fleet came out on the side of the Parliamentarians, and thereafter he fought in the Royalist armies, becoming Governor of Pendennis Castle.

In 1648, he came back to the Isle of Wight and avidly followed King Charles' fortunes as he fled from Hampton Court and sought refuge at Carisbrooke Castle. When the news reached Burley that the Island's Governor had closed the gates to the castle, turning the King from a guest into a prisoner, he acted.

Taking up the Newport town drum, he beat out a warning, calling 'For God, for King and for the people!' Gradually a crowd gathered – mostly made up of women, children and elderly people. He declared himself ready to lead a revolt to rescue

Charles from his captors. His 'army', sporting a single musket between them, were carried along by the sentiment, but then Mr Moses Read, Newport's staunchly Parliamentarian mayor, came to demand his drum back.

The protest rumbled on for the rest of the day and rumours as to its seriousness escalated. The fleet off the Island's coast was warned that it might be needed to put down a rebellion. In the event, the would-be rescuers drifted away and Captain Burley was arrested.

The captain was transported to Winchester, where he was put on trial for treason. By its nature, treason is an act against the monarch, whereas Burley was working to rescue Charles – however, this did not stop him from being found guilty and executed.

Spies at Carisbrooke Castle

By the time King Charles I set foot in Carisbrooke Castle in November 1647, he was already making plans to escape. Colonel Robert Hammond, his reluctant host, had orders from parliament to keep Charles safe, at whatever cost. For his part, Charles gave his word that he would not attempt to escape, and poor, gullible Hammond believed him. Therefore it came as a shock when the colonel learned from a committee in London that on 6 April 1648, Charles had attempted to climb through a window and had only been prevented because the bars were too narrow. As a result, Henry Firebrace, Richard Osborne, Abraham Dowcett and Silius Titus – all men that Hammond trusted implicitly – were removed.

In spite of his situation, it is doubtful whether Charles seriously considered that he might be executed at this time. Over the spring and summer of 1648, he contacted many Royalists who were prepared to risk their own lives on his behalf. He wrote letters in code, referring to his supporters by initials, and concealed messages in a hole in the wall of his chamber, to be collected by servants like Mary, the laundry maid, or an old man who stoked the fires. To his groom, he secreted notes in the finger of his gloves.

In his correspondence, Charles referred to himself as 'J', the letter used for the names of every donkey since employed to turn the water wheel in the well house at the castle.

Nobody was to be trusted at the castle. Hammond was, in turn, spied upon by certain servants in his employ – men acting as double agents and playing a dangerous game.

Other attempted escapes were plotted and discovered: a plan to take Charles out through the ceiling; to light a diversionary fire while he slipped out in disguise; and to bribe the guards.

As parliament tried to negotiate a settlement with the King, the army grew tired of his prevarication and, taking matters into their own hands, removed the King to London for trial and execution. Hammond withdrew from public life until 1654, when Oliver Cromwell had become Lord Protector. He accepted a role in Ireland, but a few weeks after his arrival he caught a fever and died.

A Clever Spy

Among the prisoners at Parkhurst Gaol in 1913 was William Klare, believed by British police to be 'one of the cleverest spies in the German Foreign Service'. Klare was a dentist working in Portsmouth, and he cultivated various friendships with dockyard personnel. One of his contacts, Levi Rosenthal, was in fact a government spy, and when he was offered $1,000 dollars by Klare to borrow a naval book, Rosenthal reported him. As a result, he was sentenced to five years in gaol for spying.

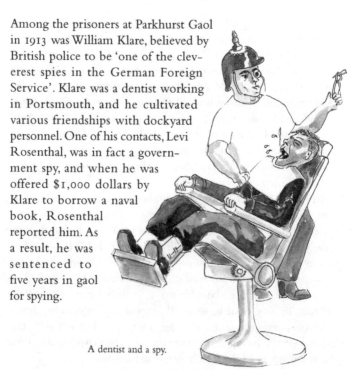

A dentist and a spy.

Chapter Four

Suffer the Little Children

The Awful Case of John Valentine Gray

The short life of little Valentine Gray is very much a part of Island history. In the early nineteenth-century, Newport was a jumble of cottages, increasingly interspersed with solid town houses; as in all urban clusters, fire was commonly feared. Chimney soot was often a factor in starting a blaze that could do untold damage, and, as a result, chimney sweeping was paramount – which is where Valentine comes into the story.

In 1812, John Valentine Gray was born and baptised in Alverstoke, Hampshire. He grew up with no memory of his mother, Mary, for by the time he was six months old she died, and Valentine was taken into the House of Industry. Compared to the alternative of dying in the gutter, it was a better choice – for the time being at least. Life was regimented, humdrum, but he was clothed and fed, and received some form of education in preparation for his future place in society.

The workhouse was always overcrowded; as soon as possible, children were moved on to begin apprenticeships and earn their keep. At the age of nine, Valentine was formally apprenticed to Benjamin Davies, a chimney sweep living in Newport on Isle of Wight. The little boy was taken from all that was familiar as he set out towards a nightmare existence of abuse.

The Davies family probably lived in Pyle St Newport. With his wife Margaret, Davis seems to have had several children and also took in lodgers. Valentine was quickly to find himself in a world where he had no idea what was expected of him, but however hard he tried, he got it wrong and was punished for his failings.

Davis had a drink problem and often took his anger out on his family. The arrival of Valentine gave him a focus for his violence; within days he was being beaten for failing to sweep chimneys to his master's satisfaction. Neighbours overheard the

The awful fate of Valentine Gray.

sounds of cries as the man's abuse was piled on the child. It was now winter, and as a punishment Valentine was turned out into the yard to wash his clothes and threatened with the hose when he dared to say that he was cold.

A chilling account told how, having gone to bed without seeking permission, exhausted, Valentine was dragged out and beaten. From being an already skinny child, he became cowed and skeletal; his hands and feet were swollen, his faced bruised and his wrists sore from being tied up.

At the beginning of November, Margaret Davis sent for Dr Buckell of Newport. He found Valentine cosily tucked up in bed. On being roused, however, the child complained of pains in his head and was diagnosed with inflammation of the brain. Upon routine examination, Buckell noted about twenty sores on his body, but in general described him as healthy. Within twenty-four hours he was back at the house, and it was clear that Valentine was close to death. When he died the following day, a subsequent, more thorough examination revealed that his entire body was covered in sores and bruises.

An inquest was held at Newport's Guildhall and although a blow to the head was identified as the fatal wound, it was not possible to say for certain whether or not Benjamin Davis inflicted it. He and Margaret were arrested and sent to Winchester to await trial on a count of manslaughter. They appeared at the Lent Assizes in 1822, where fifteen witnesses attested to Valentine being left naked in the yard, spread-eagled on a table to be beaten, punched, whipped and generally tortured.

At the end of the trial, Margaret Davies was found not guilty and her husband guilty of manslaughter. Although he went to gaol, it seems that it was not for the crime of hurting Valentine, but because he failed to pay a fine of 1s.

Murder at Parkhurst Barracks Field

It was a Friday afternoon at the end of August 1898, and nine-year-old Percy Hayter of Albert Cottages, Worsley Road, Newport had gone out to play. It was the last day of the school holidays, and unknown to Percy's family, the last day of his life. Within a few hours, his body was discovered in Parkhurst Barrack Field with his throat cut.

The alarm was raised when forty-two-year-old Maurice Holbrook, who had until recently been incarcerated in Newport Workhouse, walked into the police station and gave himself up, saying that he had killed a child. He produced a bloodstained penknife and he had blood on his hands and clothes. On investigation, Percy's body was found in Parkhurst Barracks Field about 4 yards from the hedge, shielded from view along the Yarmouth Road.

Percy was carried to the infirmary at the workhouse, and the following morning, in an atmosphere of heightened emotion, an inquest was held. Poor Susannah Hayter, Percy's mother, was called upon to identify him and explain when she had last seen her son, which had been at about one o'clock the previous day. Her husband Harry, a labourer at the cement works, was at her side.

As soon as news of the murder reached the neighbourhood, a hostile crowd gathered outside the courthouse and Holbrook was forced to run the gauntlet of their anger. He was whisked away and detained in Kingston Prison (at Portsmouth).

A hearing took place at Newport's Guildhall. The court was full of avid members of the public, and, to avoid a repeat of the angry scenes before, the accused travelled earlier than the expected time. He was described as gaunt and weak, with an air of apparent indifference. When questioned, he answered in monosyllables and his voice was barely audible.

Poor, sobbing Susannah Hayter gave evidence. Also called was thirteen-year-old George Armstrong, who had been playing with Percy that afternoon. He and other boys had left the field because it began to rain, but Percy had remained behind. They last saw him swinging on a tree. His body was found close to that spot.

Thirteen-year-old Albert Ledicott of Crocker Street had been playing with some other boys and had seen Holbrook heading towards the field at about ten minutes to one. The prisoner had started to come towards them and they had run away. At about 2.35 p.m. another witness, Charles Salter, had seen Holbrook leaving the field by way of a wicket gate.

When questioned, Holbrook said that he did not know what had made him do it but that he had not eaten for three days. He was committed to the next Assizes and removed to Winchester Gaol.

A memorial service was held on Sunday evening at the Salvation Army Barracks, where Percy had played the cornet. His funeral took place the following Tuesday afternoon. His coffin, covered in flowers, was taken from his home accompanied by his parents, brother and sisters, members of the Salvation Army, neighbours, school mates, playmates and members of the Juvenile Foresters, of which he had been a member. Amid the flowers on the coffin was his cornet. Mr Ledicott of The Old Curiosity Shop in Newport started a collection to erect a memorial to Percy in the cemetery.

Meanwhile, Holbrook was found guilty of the murder but was declared insane and ordered to be detained at Her Majesty's Pleasure.

Early Child Deaths Reported to the Coroner

Coroners' Courts were certainly in existence in the thirteenth century and a few early records survive, showing that infant mortality was all too familiar. In the fourteenth century, four Isle of Wight children met unhappy deaths by falling into wells. These children have their names recorded for posterity.

John Favell was just aged two-and-a-half when he fell into a wayside well when out playing with his hoop at Stanwell, part of Bembridge. His body was discovered by his mother.

At Newchurch, two-year-old Helen, daughter of John Couherd, fell into a well. Again, it was her poor mother that discovered the tragedy.

Juliana, the two-year-old daughter of John Breketo, had been playing in a field when she too fell into a well, this one belonging to Simon Someres. It seems that his wife made the awful discovery.

John, son of Richard atte Hulle was only eighteen months old when he met a similar fate.

Whether the parents could be blamed for the deaths is open to question. They almost certainly would have blamed themselves.

Two incidents involving scalding also came to the coroner's attention. At Wroxall, two-and-a-half-year-old William Way was fatally scalded by the contents of a boiling cauldron heating over the fire, while John Elof died when a pan of water scalded his back. In the tradition of the time, the pan, as the cause of death, was valued at 4*d*.

More than 400 years later, similar tragedies were being recorded. The number and frequency makes chilling reading. Often, the reason how and why a child died were never identified:

1850: George William Kennett, aged ten months, was accidentally scalded.

7 March 1851: An inquisition was held on the body of a newborn female child at Shide. Verdict: found dead.

8 Aug 1851: Female child about one year at Mottistone. Cause of death: unknown.

Between 1852 and 1853, the following catalogue of child deaths were recorded:

6 February: A newborn child at Newport found dead – no evidence.

1 June: Mary Williams, four years. Verdict: accidental death.

5 June: Thorness Farm, Eliza Attrill, three months eight days – died by visitation of God.

30 June: Mary Ann Coggen of Cross Lane, eight years six months – accidentally burned.

24 July: Archibald Henry Campbell at Seaview, seven years ten month – accidentally drowned.

5 August: James Cook, North Fairlee, six years eleven months – found drowned.

3 September: Harriet Woodford of Carisbrooke, five years five months – accidental death.

20 September: Sarah Colenutt of Niton, three years – accidentally smothered.

27 September: Henry Nicholas of Ventnor, twelve years – accidental death.

30 September: Louisa Elizabeth Arnold, four years – accidentally burnt.

1 Oct: Charles Edward Shotter, East Cowes, three years six months – found drowned.

12 April: Dennis, West Cowes, aged four weeks and four days, found dead but cause of death unknown.

11 March: Harriet Floyd, Cowes, three years – accidental death.

In some cases there was little doubt that a crime had been committed. On 27 October 1859, the coroner reported on the body of a newborn male child – 'born alive but immediately afterwards suffocated' in Ryde. Previous to this, on 16 October, the body of the illegitimate child of Eliza Humby was discovered in Ryde. The verdict was that the injuries to the head had been caused by the child 'accidentally falling to the floor'.

In a particularly dramatic case, on 22 October 1901, Samuel Georges Hughes, aged two, and Annie Louisa Hughes, aged thirty-five, were killed by Sam Hughes, aged twenty-seven, who then committed suicide.

Young People Nowadays!

Local newspapers reported the following cases of mischief:

8 June 1829: Two local boys named Wadham and Cass were convicted at the Petty Sessions for cutting down and attempting to steal away timber from a coppice belonging to Sir Fitzwilliam Barrington Bart. They were fined £5 each but being unable to pay, were committed to the bridewell for two months with exercise in the treadmill.

The theft of two cheeses – cheddar or Stilton?

January 1874: Albert Bartlett and Kenneth Arnold, both aged twelve, of St Helens, were charged with stealing ¾lb of cheese from Mrs Calloway's shop. Dubbed 'very bad boys', they were each sentenced to seven days' hard labour in Winchester Prison, and six strokes of the birch to be received 'privately'.

Prior to 1948, the use of the birch as corporal punishment was permissible, and children could receive up to twelve strokes. Curiously, this chastisement could only be applied to boys under the age of fourteen. So when three local lads, Frederick Poland, Frank Flaxmer and Harry Tribbick, were convicted of stealing some swede-tops, they all claimed to be over fourteen years of age. Judging by their size, the court decided that Flaxman and Tribbick were not fourteen and were, therefore, sentenced to six lashes each. Poland, who was clearly above that age, was fined 5s. The magistrates concurred that he too deserved a whipping.

Because of the perceived rise in juvenile crime during the First World War, the question of raising the age at which whipping could be used as a punishment was referred by the Island's

Standing Joint Committee to the Home Office. Inevitably, two opposing views were aired. Mr Hayden, later Chief Constable, questioned whether anyone could seriously believe that corporal punishment prevented crime; what was needed, he said, was an approach that addressed the cause of crime. Mr Fellowes voiced the view that young blackguards 'richly deserved' a thrashing which they would never forget.

Juvenile Smugglers

Although children were often, no doubt, acting under the orders of adults, they were not spared the punishment that fitted the crime.

Little Caroline Tizzard of Portsea, just nine years old, was arrested for carrying two six-gallon tubs of brandy. The weight alone must have been terrific, but Caroline was fined £5. Unable to pay, she was committed to the Common Gaol in Newport for one month.

Perhaps worse was the treatment of Henry Lane, aged twelve, of School Green Road, Freshwater. He was accused of harbouring and concealing con-traband goods and was fined £100. The fine was then reduced to £50 but, of course, he could not pay, so he was committed to the Common Gaol at Winchester until such time as the penalty was paid. I wonder if he ever got out.

The Parkhurst Boys

The complex generally referred to as Parkhurst was built in 1778, as a hospital to serve the adjoining barracks. In 1838, the authorities decided to use the former army hospital as a juvenile reformatory for boys up to the age of fifteen. It was a solution to the pressing problem of what to do with young offenders.

Their stay, however, was only intended as a temporary one. The general message was 'Go south young man!' and after evaluating their characters, they were to be transported. In the meantime, bad boys were being housed in ever more crowded, rotting prison ships, known as hulks.

When Captain James Cook discovered a whole new continent, ripe for development, the process of emptying the hulks and carting the residents to the Antipodes began. From 1787, for the next eighty years, 160,000 men, women and children were despatched across the world, the majority never to return.

In the eighteenth and nineteenth centuries, concerns for the future of ten-year-old hardened criminals – and even the unfortunate adult who wasn't really bad, only poor – were voiced. Why not allow the better sort of criminal to start a new life, well away from Europe, provided he would work for decent folk out there and promise not to come back before his sentence had been served? To this end, in 1844, Queen Victoria issued the following directive:

> We, in consideration of some circumstances humbly represented unto us, are graciously pleased to extend our mercy and grace unto them and to grant them our pardon for which they stand convicted. On condition, they do remain and continue within our Australian Territories whether they are about to be sent in pursuance of their respective sentences, for and during the remaining term of such respective sentence.

In the meantime, the young miscreants waited on the Isle of Wight.

Parkhurst Juvenile Reformatory

It was not until 1838 that the law was amended to separate child prisoners from adults. As a result, Parkhurst Military Hospital closed its doors and then opened them as Parkhurst Juvenile Reformatory.

In his book *A Topographical and Historical Guide to the Isle of Wight*, Thomas Brettell described how a portion of the barracks at

Parkhurst was assigned by the government as a general penitentiary for juvenile offenders. Here, under taskmasters, the young
inmates were to be taught useful skills. The number of prisoners
was to be 250. The cost of running the penitentiary for the year
ending March 1841 was £5,807.

On Boxing Day 1838, the first Governor, Robert Woolcombe,
and a supporting team arrived at Parkhurst to take charge of
102 boys. Whilst awaiting transportation, many were employed
making and moulding bricks to build two new prison wings.
They worked in silence and carried out mindless tasks such as
oakum picking. Corporal punishment was routine. Unruly boys
were locked up and constrained with strait jackets.

By 1842, the young offenders began their
adventure into the unknown. On 20 April
1842, the ship *Simon Tailor* carried 245
passengers for Freemantle. On board
were eighteen Parkhurst boys; many
more were to follow.

The Australians did not take the
new flood of immigration lying
down. The colony of Auckland was
founded with the understanding
that no convicts should be settled
there but on 25 October 1842,
the barque *St George* arrived
with ninety-two boys
on board. They had
been trained as
shoemakers and
tailors – neither
skill being par-
ticularly desired.

Three weeks later the
vessel *Mandarin* arrived with
thirty-one boys, this time trained in
carpentry and building. Although some found
employment, they were treated harshly and many
were shipped to the copper mines, where they fared

little better than slaves. Others worked on the roads, many didn't even have shoes to protect their feet.

The 1841 census shows that at least 111 boys were in Parkhurst. The youngest, James Goodrich, was just eleven.

The First Murder Down Under

Perhaps the burgeoning Australian colonies were right to fear the arrival of known criminals, for in 1844 the first murder by a European on the continent was carried out by Parkhurst boy John Gavin, who, in a fit of rage, killed his employer's fifteen-year-old son, George Pollard, with an axe.

Gavin had been sentenced at Warwick in 1840 for larceny and for being a Chartist, for which he got ten years. He was thirteen years old. He arrived in Australia on board the ship *Shepherd* in October 1843. He had been shipped out with 234 other young offenders.

His trial took place on 3 April 1844 and he was sentenced to death in Perth. He was publicly hanged in front of the Round House in Freemantle that same year.

In 1845, Queen Victoria visited Parkhurst and liked what she saw. The boys appeared smart and polite, dutifully serenading her with the national anthem. She was so moved that she granted pardons to two of the boys, who were each awarded two-year apprenticeships.

Meanwhile, the happy state of life inside was not quite what it seemed. The coroners' book recorded the following boys' deaths in Parkhurst:

The first execution down under.

1852

3 September: Patrick Hart, sixteen years two months – accidental death.

27 September: Thomas Fitzpatrick, fifteen years seven months – natural death.

15 November: Thomas Ryan, sixteen years nine months – natural death.

1 December: Thomas Cassidy, seventeen years – natural death.

1853

14 January: David Martin, seventeen years – natural death.

26 April: Jacob Weston, eighteen years nine months – natural death.

25 August: William King, eighteen years – visitation of God.
2 November: Stewart Ogilvie, age unknown – natural death.

1854
1 March: Jeremiah Daley, eighteen years – natural death.
18 March: Elias Moses, eighteen years – natural death.

1855
28 February: George Rivett, sixteen years – natural death.
Patrick Battle at Parkhurst Prison, aged eighteen – taking
poison with intent to produce sickness.

The most common cause of death was consumption. During
1837–8, five boys died of the disease. Inadequate food, the cold,
savage punishments and general despair must have played a part.

The boys might have seemed good and biddable to Queen
Victoria, but given half a chance they were over the wall and away.
The *Isle of Wight Observer* of 15 June 1851 reported, 'The escape
by one or more of these juveniles has become such an ordinary
occurrence that the public have got used to it.'

When it came to transportation, it was decreed that boys under
the age of fifteen should not be shipped overseas. Unfortunately
for them, they were to be held at Parkhurst until they reached that
age, and only then would they begin their sentences. In effect, a
twelve-year-old sentenced to seven years' transportation actually
served ten years.

Some people criticised the system for giving the young offenders secure accommodation and regular food – a luxury denied
to many children outside who were homeless, alone and hungry.

The Theft of Two Loaves

The Old Bailey tried the following children who were thought
to be deserving of transportation.

William Wren was thirteen years old when he appeared on a
charge of simple larceny – the theft of two loaves of bread valued

Thou shalt not steal.

at 10*d* – the property of John Coutts. Another boy, John Lucker, was employed by Coutts to deliver bread, and in court he swore that when he was in Kensington Square, between two and three o'clock on 14 November 1838, he left his basket for five minutes and returned to find two loaves missing. He saw the prisoner about 100 yards away and approached him, finding the bread in his possession. He had not seen him before. Wren was found guilty and sentenced to seven years' transportation.

James Goodall was fourteen years old when he was arrested for stealing a handkerchief valued at 4*s*. A passer-by noticed one boy touch the coat of a man in the street and pass something to a companion. The first boy ran away but James was apprehended, and although the event took place in a crowded street, the witness swore that James was the boy receiving the stolen goods. Ann Lane, a laundress, came forward to give James a good character, but he was found guilty and sentenced to ten years' transportation.

In the first ten years, nearly 1,500 boys were transported in this way.

Report on the Juvenile Prison at Parkhurst, 1866

By this date, all juvenile prisoners were being removed from Parkhurst, either because they were discharged or because they had grown into men. The boys were sent to other prisons and a special class had been formed for young juveniles at Portland.

During the nineteenth century, escape from Parkhurst was a regular event, although most escapees were recaptured within a day. Typical was Henry Hamstead, who took advantage of the fog to abscond but was recaptured a day later at Kitbridge Farm, less than a mile away. He was so hungry that he was found raiding the pig bin for food.

In 1931, twelve junior offenders managed to escape from Parkhurst and get to the mainland.

As Parkhurst closed its doors on its child prisoners, another group was ready to take their place. On 19 February 1863, Parkhurst opened its doors to 150 females.

Spare a final thought for John O'Connor, a baby aged four weeks. He was taken from the prison ship where he died on 6 August 1816, and was buried at Whippingham.

Chapter Five

The Female of the Species

The Island's Only Saint

One of the Island's earliest documented murders was carried out by a woman. In the early thirteenth century, Amicia Norri, daughter of Hugh de Norays, was married to Simon of Atherfield. In March 1211, Simon died and, at first, it was thought that he

was killed during a French attack on the Island, but on 21 March 1211, Amicia was reportedly charged with killing him.

Why or how he died is not recorded, but, not long after his demise, reports of miracles began to circulate, inspiring local people to make pilgrimages to his tomb. Over the months, pilgrims visiting his grave left donations to the value of £7. His martyrdom was recorded at Gonville and Caius College Cambridge, and, in 1211, he became St Simon.

For whatever reason, the cult of St Simon was short lived – possibly suppressed by the Bishop of Winchester, who found it not to his liking.

As for Amicia, she was accused of petty treason and found guilty. She suffered the agonising death of being burned at the stake. Simon was recorded as being 'a martyr to his wife' – or should that be the other way round?

Roast Rector, Anyone?

Who knows what was going through the mind of Lady Anne Worsley when she accused Thomas Bradshaw, the vicar of All Saints' Church at Godshill, of trying to poison her?

'I don't trust that vicar – his sermons are poisonous.'

Anne was a part of the powerful Leigh family, and her marriage to James Worsley of Appuldurcombe made her status even higher, for her husband was keeper of King Henry VII's wardrobe, Keeper of the Beasts in the Tower of London, and Captain of the Island. He had been granted these titles following his unenviable childhood job of being whipping boy for the future King Henry VIII.

In 1531, Anne accused Revd Bradshaw of conspiring to poison her with one of the servants in her household. She further claimed that another household member had already been despatched by the pair. What evidence there might have been is unknown, but so determined was the good lady to prove her case that the accusation was referred to the King. Happily for Thomas Bradshaw, the King dismissed the charge, warning Worsley that his wife should desist from her campaign. Had the charge been proved, Bradshaw would have suffered the fate of other poisoners – to be boiled in oil.

Saying You're Sorry?

On 21 March 1788, Elizabeth Cushen of East Cowes made a public declaration of her guilt and remorse in the *Salisbury and Winchester Journal*:

> I, Elizabeth Cushen, having experienced the lenity of the gentlemen who were lately robbed of flour from the vessel *Nancy* in Newport River, which I purchased at a price no ways adequate to its value, of Charles George, now under sentence of transportation for seven years for robbing the said vessel, do hereby acknowledge my very blameable conduct in dealing for the said flour with a person so suspicious and unjust...

Bad Mothers?

At first glance, women who found themselves in court often came across as uncaring, inept mothers but their actions were often driven by desperation.

With illegitimacy regarded as sinful, and no provision made for childcare while a woman worked, many a frantic mother abandoned or killed her baby at birth.

The *Hampshire Telegraph* on 5 August 1839, reported on an inquest held at Swainston on the body of a newborn infant found in the privy. It was identified as being the child of a laundress, Mary Mew, and had been born a fortnight earlier. The baby had a cord about its neck, indicating that it had been strangled.

When questioned, other members of staff denied any knowledge of the event; they claimed to not even know that Mew had been pregnant. The magistrates decided that Mew should be charged not with infanticide but with concealing the birth. On 30 September, however, she appeared before the county court charged with murdering the baby.

The majority of sentences concerning the suspicious deaths of newborn infants were mercifully tempered with compassion, so hopefully Mary suffered no worse than a spell in prison – as if that would not have been painful enough. Other similar cases were recorded locally.

On 12 January 1852, at the Coroner's Court in Newport, Frances (Fanny) Groundsell was charged with the wilful murder of her newborn female child. The case was heard at Winchester, where Fanny was instead found guilty of concealing the birth of the child and sentenced to six months in gaol.

On 22 January 1863, Ann Snow was charged with the wilful murder of her newborn female child at the Needles Hotel. She was tried at Winchester, where the charge was changed to 'attempting to conceal the birth of a child', for which she received a sentence of one year in prison.

On 3 October 1902, Charles Gawn, aged four years, was drowned by his mother, Jane Gardner, in Ryde, while she was temporarily insane. The same Jane then drowned herself.

The Case of Frances Stallard

In many ways, the case of Frances Stallard was not exceptional; what was unusual was the public response to her trial.

In 1856, Annette Stallard gave birth to the sixth of her seven children, a girl whom she called Frances. Annette and her husband George, an agricultural labourer, had both been born at Chale, where Frances first saw the light of day.

When Frances was eighteen, she became romantically involved with a shipwright named George Gatrell. George was working at Lymington but his family was local. He was fifteen years older than Frances and, no doubt, glamorous and persuasive in her eyes. She soon became pregnant. When she told him, he promptly left the country, leaving Frances to face the consequences. As a result, she was sent to the House of Industry, where, in January 1875, she gave birth to a daughter whom she named Agnes Ellen.

Of all the residents in the House of Industry, unmarried mothers were the most despised; their names were entered in a black book and they were forced to wear rough yellow garments to distinguish them from the poor but 'decent' women.

When baby Agnes was five months old, Frances was sent out to work and Agnes was farmed out to be looked after. After some time, Frances received a message to say that Agnes was being neglected and that she should go and fetch her. Accordingly, she and her mother Annette immediately set out from Chale to fetch the little girl home. They faced a terrible discovery. Agnes, now two years old, was unable to sit unaided or to walk, and had frequent haemorrhages from her nose and ears. Clearly she had been brutally treated and was suffering some brain damage.

Caring for the disabled child must have been difficult, and after four weeks Frances announced that she was taking Agnes to the parents of George Gatrell, who lived at Wroxall, and that they were going to look after her. She set off and later returned without her daughter. Shortly afterwards, Agnes was found drowned in a stream. When challenged, Frances said that she had killed her by putting a cloth over her face because she would not stop crying.

Frances was tried before Lord Coleridge who, having heard the evidence, doffed the black cap and sentenced Frances to death.

There must have been something about the girl, for there was an immediate local outcry, which then became national, and bowing to pressure, her sentence was commuted to life in prison. She was sent to Knaphill Gaol at Woking.

Knaphill opened in 1858 and housed prisoners with mental and physical disabilities. Here there was some attempt to rehabilitate the women, many of whom worked at breaking marble to make fish-scale mosaic floors. They received a small wage of up to 1s 2d a day.

Thanks to a book written by a Mrs Houston, *Only a Woman's Life*, a campaign for Frances' release began and she left the gaol in 1889.

In spite of her past, Frances slotted back into ordinary life. In 1891 she found work as a servant at 23 George Street, Ryde, in the house of Alice Alcock, who described herself as a 'scholastic'. Frances was listed as single and aged thirty-two. In 1901, she was housekeeper to Mr Salter, a general labourer and widower at 6 Birkbeck Cottages, Avenue Road, Sandown. She lived until 1927, when she died aged seventy-six. Her death was registered in the Cowes district.

The Sorry Tale of Anne Jolliffe

In June 1915, Anne Jolliffe was put on trial at Winchester for the manslaughter of her baby son Charles Rowland.

Charles was born in February in a Salvation Army home in London, where Anne's angry parents had despatched her on discovering her pregnancy. After the baby's birth, she was sent back home to her parents at Yafford. She was full of trepidation, knowing that she was still in disgrace.

Arriving at Portsmouth, she looked out for her parents but they were not there to meet her. At Ryde they also failed to appear and, in despair, Anne boarded the train to carry her home. Unable to face the prospect of their wrath, as the train went through the tunnel at Ryde, Anne dropped baby Charles from the window. He was discovered some time later. In the opinion of the coroner, he had died not from injuries following the fall but from exposure.

In Anne's defence, the lawyer stated that she had never intended to harm her son, but hoped that someone would find him and take care of him. In the face of her extreme distress and the circumstances of the case, Anne was found guilty of manslaughter and sentenced to twelve months' imprisonment.

The Case of Mary Ellen Queenan

On 16 June 1906, Mary Ellen Queenan, a hawker of Newport, was accused of deserting her children in a tenement in Sea Street. Described as living in a shed, the children – aged thirteen, seven and five – were found in filthy conditions with no food or heating. They had not seen their mother for two days. The children were removed to the workhouse and Mary was picked up in Portsmouth, where she claimed that she was looking for a house. In her defence, she said she had been married to an army pensioner at the age of fourteen, from whom she had parted; she had raised fifteen children without a husband to support her. She swore that she loved her children more than her own life.

Mary had recently been living with another man and had a baby with him. They also parted, but the man was eventually willing to take her back. She swore that it would break her baby's heart if she were to be imprisoned. Seemingly unmoved, the Bench sentenced her to one month in gaol with hard labour.

Immoral Earnings

Following Mary Queenan into the court was Jane Langam of Orchard Street, Newport, accused of using her house as a brothel. Jane, an altogether feistier woman, was separated from her husband and complained, loudly, that she was being spied on by the police. Stoutly, she declared that she would not suggest the officers were liars but that one 'had a false pair of jaws'.

Jane challenged their right to interfere if she chose to entertain male friends, but the magistrates took a dim view and sentenced her to one month's hard labour.

On 19 January 1929, Mrs Amelia Emma Dyer, a widow, appeared in court charged with prostituting her daughter, Florence, who was thirteen years old. Amelia took in laundry from the barracks and frequently took her daughter with her. She was accused of inviting soldiers to her house.

On 7 December, the year before, Florence had given birth to a child. Amelia claimed that she had no idea that the girl was pregnant. In her defence, she stated that she never left Florence alone with a soldier for more than half an hour.

An innocent abroad?

Five soldiers were known to have frequented the house, but were not called as witnesses. Florence and the baby were taken into the care of the Isle of Wight Preventive and Rescue Society, and her mother was sent for trial at the Assizes.

Women and Smuggling

In view of its lucrative nature, women were naturally involved in smuggling and, in turn, prosecuted. Their full skirts made concealing contraband easier, and they were less likely to be searched.

Diana Hudson of West Cowes was prosecuted on 15 April 1824 for being in possession of 15½lbs of coffee, on which no duty had been paid. Being her first offence, the accrued penalty was £6 15s but it was reduced by two thirds, and on 8 May Diana paid up.

In May 1825, Elizabeth Wright, Sarah Wright and Elizabeth Tribbeck, all of St Helens, were prosecuted for being in possession of gin on which no duty had been paid. Having children at home, Elizabeth seems to have been given time to pay the penalty of £6 15s, but Elizabeth and Ann both failed to appear in court and would have had to pay the full amount – or face gaol.

In December 1832, Ann Southcott, Jemima Stallard and Ann Skinner were all prosecuted for concealing a quantity of tubs in their houses. The £100 fine was mitigated to one quarter for Southcott and Stallard, but as they could not pay, they were committed to gaol. Ann Skinner failed to appear in court so was charged the full penalty.

In May 1835, Mary Ann Matthews was found to be carrying and conveying 4 gallons of foreign brandy. She was fined £100 but, in default of payment, ended up being committed for six months' hard labour at Winchester House of Correction.

In September/October 1835, Elizabeth Stone, Matilda Green and Matilda Street were all discovered with skins of foreign spirits (mostly gin – called geneva). Each was sentenced to serve six months in Winchester, but without hard labour.

On 13 December 1838, Mary Gutteridge was fined £5 for carrying a ¾ gallon of brandy. She was fined £5 but failed to pay, and so was sent to the Common Gaol at Newport for one month.

The Scandal of Sophie Dawes

Sophie Dawes is viewed, along with Michal Morey, as one of the Island's most celebrated villains. Sophie was born around 1791 in the tiny fishing village of St Helens. Her father, Dicky, was a local rogue who made a living from smuggling and then drank away the profits.

Exhausted by the struggle to survive, Sophie's mother Jane Calloway went into the workhouse to prevent her children from starving. Here, Sophie was trained in domestic service. At the age of fourteen, the child was sent out to work, but she quickly discovered that domestic servitude was not for her. She ran away and crossed the water, first to Portsmouth and then to London, where she found work as a maid in a brothel.

Here, she came to the attention of the exiled French duke Louis Henri, Prince de Conde and Duc de Bourbon. At this time, Louis was fifty-six and Sophie around twenty-three. Following the execution of his kinsman, King Louis XVI of France, Louis had fled to England and was kicking his heels, waiting for the time when he could go back home. Sophie, with her earthy attraction and ignorance, amused him, so he set about refining her, teaching her French, Latin, Greek and music. He also set her up as his mistress in a house at Turnham Green in London.

Sophie must have thought that she was made for life, but Louis suddenly returned to France, leaving her behind. He would not have given her a second thought, but she was not prepared to be cast aside so easily, and so followed him.

At this time, the remnants of the French court were quite puritanical; a mistress from the gutter was not what Louis needed. The resourceful Sophie, however, let it be known that she was Conde's daughter and hoodwinked a member of the Royal Guard, Adrien Victor de Feucheres, into marrying her. He was made a baron, giving Sophie the title Baronne de Feucheres; she now had legitimate access to the prince. When Feucheres realised what was happening, he withdrew from the court, but by this time Sophie had worked her feminine wiles and Louis was convinced that he was in love with her. Shielded by his title, she remained in his company.

Sophie was astute enough to realise that her charms would not last, and so she began to extort money and property from the besotted Conde. When wheedling did not work, she bullied him and slowly isolated him from his family and peers. She took his family jewels and succeeded in separating him totally from his daughter, Madame de Rully. She brought members of her own family to live with her, installing her mother and sister, Charlotte, in a house in Paris, while her sister Matilda and brother James (who she passed off as a nephew) became part of Conde's household.

The isolated and ageing prince made James his equerry and his companion. He was found a noble wife and the title Baron de Flassons was purchased for him. Bit by bit, Louis transferred his wealth and lands to Sophie, but, realising that the French court would never tolerate her as sole beneficiary of his will, she entered into an agreement with the Duc d'Orleans, persuading Louis to make the duke's son his adoptive heir.

Beaten and humiliated, Louis realised that once the will was signed, his mistress would have no further use for him and he made increasingly desperate attempts to escape. On 26 August 1830, he planned to flee from her clutches.

The night before, he and Sophie played cards, both seeming in a buoyant mood, but the next morning he did not appear. He was soon found hanging from the crossbar of a window. A verdict of suicide was given, even though the old duke was so infirm that he could not raise his hands high enough to dress his hair. To reveal the truth, however, would have exposed a scandal too great to risk.

In theory, Sophie now had everything she wanted, but the French court denied her a coveted place in society. Increasingly outcast, she decided to sell up and retreat to England.

The scandalous Sophie Dawes

On the journey home, her nephew James, who had been a party to events at Conde's palace, mysteriously fell ill and died. In spite of a surgeon's conviction that it was not apoplexy, as suggested, no autopsy was carried out. The general feeling was that James had been poisoned to keep him quiet. Sophie had his body returned to the Isle of Wight, where he was buried in St Helens churchyard.

Sophie bought herself an estate called Bure Homage, outside of Christchurch in Hampshire, and a London house in Hyde Park Square. Her mother, always devout, entered a convent. Sophie named her sister Charlotte's child, also named Sophie, as her heir.

Perhaps with a belated burst of conscience, Sophie lived out her final years converting to Catholicism and giving money to charity. She died on 15 December 1840 from a heart attack. As her biographer Marjorie Bowen so graphically put it, 'She was stifled quickly as if strangled by an invisible hand.'

Her unsigned will caused dispute and in an ironic act of justice, much of the French money passed to her estranged husband Adrien de Feucheres.

Bad Girls

On 19 February 1863, the staff at Parkhurst Prison were awaiting the arrival of 150 female prisoners. The gaols at Millbank and Brixton were being updated, and the last Parkhurst boys were about to leave, making it a suitable place to house them until the new arrangements were complete.

The women were coming with female members of staff, but if the existing warders thought that women would be easier – more manageable – they were in for a shock.

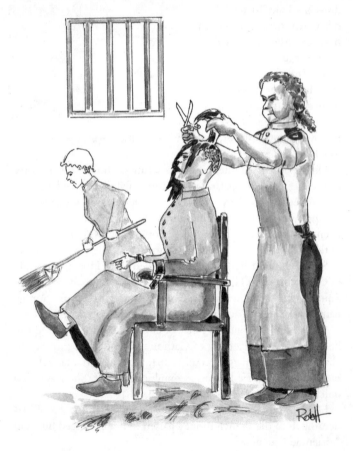

In the year that the women arrived, journalist Frederick Robinson wrote, 'There is not a man to match the worst inmates of our female prisons… punishment has no effect, save to bring them to death's door – and we must let them have their way or see them die.'

Mary Carpenter, an authority on female felons, also confirmed that, when upset, 'women go madly to work at everything breakable and tearable within range'. Any regime designed to break their spirits had the potential to go badly wrong.

On 7 May, another forty women arrived and were unloaded at Commercial Wharf, while on 16 July a further thirty women were disembarked. It was confidently predicted that women prisoners would continue to arrive until the gaol was full.

On the surface, prison life at Parkhurst would seem to be more conducive than that at Millbank, which was a dark, damp, gloomy monolith. The same rules applied, however. The women had their hair cut short, although many fought against it. They were dressed in brown serge frocks with white caps. Most of their time was spent in solitude and their work was sedentary. It allowed them to brood on the fact that, when released, they would invariably return to the same hopeless situation that had brought them there.

Not long after their arrival, Queen Victoria graced the prison with a visit. Some years before, she had also dropped in to inspect the boy prisoners; so well behaved did she find them that she arranged two pardons. If she arrived expecting more of the same, she was in for a shock.

For a start, the women presented a resentful, brooding presence. Many insisted on turning their backs on her and they resolutely refused to sing the national anthem. When she left, the Queen promptly decreed that no member of the royal family was to set foot in the prison again.

It was after her departure that things really went wrong. Wound up by the visit, the women rioted, some breaking out into the prison yard where they tore off their clothes and refused to come in. Against their wrath, the female wardens were helpless. They eventually had to call upon the neighbouring menfolk to come to their aid. Initially they declined, but, in view of the seriousness of the situation, it was decreed that only married officers would

Only the married men dare approach.

approach the naked rebels. Eventually, armed with blankets and hose-pipes, they managed to subdue the rioters and restore order.

In the following year, 223 new prisoners arrived plus a further 143 re-convictions – mostly for larceny or common theft. In fact, in 1865, eighty-three per cent of convictions among females were for larceny. In that year, 402 females were discharged on licence, one was pardoned, four were sent to a lunatic asylum, thirty-four were released at the end of their sentence, fifteen died, and forty-one were sent to the new Carlisle Memorial Refuge at Bloomsbury.

Giving the high incidence of re-offending, the causes were listed as: a general sense of worthlessness following frequent sentencing; the inability to find work; and the bad influence of friends. No doubt, women were also driven to thieve to feed their children.

Some Island Bad Girls

Not all the female villains were behind bars in Parkhurst, however. The following women found themselves up before the Bench for various misdemeanours.

In October 1864, Sarah and Louise Hardy, of Paradise Row at Ryde, were jointly charged for using indecent and profane language to Caroline Elizabeth James in the street. They were fined 5s.

June 1861 saw Rosina Hawkes, of Oakfield Ryde, charged with stealing a gold watch from Mr Alfred Francis Gibbs. Found guilty, she was sentenced to two months' hard labour.

In March 1879, Elizabeth Buxey, a young woman of about eighteen years old, was arrested for stealing a cloth jacket and serge dress from Louisa Turner of Somerset House, Dover Street, in Ryde. The items were valued at 15s. The defendant did not deny the charge, but pleaded that having no money, and not knowing what to do, she walked into the house and took them. She was sentenced to one month's hard labour

Sisterly love is not always obvious. Matilda Rhodes summoned her sister Jane Groves of West Cowes for wilful damage. Jane had put her fist through five panes of glass at Matilda's house; she defended herself by claiming that she had been pushed through the window by a man. When arrested, she was reported to say, 'Give my love to my sister and tell her that I'm ready to do six months for her.' The broken glass was valued at 3s and Jane was fined 3s damages and 9s costs.

Even in death, the lower classes didn't always get their names in the papers. That honour went to their superiors. Hence the death of a young servant girl was reported as 'belonging' to Mrs Litton of Egypt, near Cowes. The unnamed girl drowned in the sea of despair. According to the *Salisbury and Winchester Journal* of 12 November 1775, 'A love affair, we hear, was the cause of this rash action.' We have to feel sorry for Mrs Litton, who was inconvenienced by the thoughtlessness of her employee.

The journal was not averse to passing on the odd piece of tittle-tattle. In the same issue, it reported that Miss M***n, daughter of Anton M***n Esq of Newport – a lady with a genteel fortune – had gone off with a waiter from the Sun Inn. It was supposed that they had 'taken a trip to Scotland'; presumably to jump over the anvil and return respectably married.

Persistent Offenders

In December 1825, Elizabeth Cooper was up before the beak for concealing contraband spirits. She was the sister of Phillip

Cooper, who faced similar offences and was sent to Winchester. The reporter observed, 'Although the family of Cooper is not an extensive one, our bridewell is seldom without one of them.'

The Great Poison Pen Scandal

It had all the ingredients of an Agatha Christie novel: an English village, a choirmaster, a femme fatale, dozens of anonymous letters and a postmistress.

A scurrilous outbreak of poison pen letters started in Brighstone in 1930, after the arrival of Miss Willoughby, an unmarried village schoolmistress. Also a leading light in the church choir, Miss Willoughby no doubt came into contact with many of the village men, and she began to receive anonymous letters calling her a husband-stealer – and worse. The rector even found his name mentioned.

Gradually the recipients of these letters multiplied and the police set about trying to set a trap with the help of Mrs Creeth, the postmistress. For whatever reason, she failed to follow the instruction of the constabulary and instead of supplying specially marked stamps to those on the list of suspects, she sold them to others.

Poor Miss Willoughby could take no more and left the village, finding another position on the mainland. She left no forwarding address but later contacted the central post office at Newport, asking for any mail to be sent on to her. Not long afterwards, her new headmistress received a letter announcing that Miss Willoughby was a husband snatcher and that notice should be publicly displayed with the information.

A handwriting expert was called in, and although the writing was evidently disguised, suspicion began to fall on Mrs Creeth herself. When Miss Willoughby had written to Newport requesting her mail, she could not have known that the letter would be forwarded to Brighstone.

In her defence, Mrs Creeth stated that she too had been a recipient of the offending letters so could not be the perpetrator, but when asked to produce them, it seemed that none of them had actually gone through the postal system.

Piecing all the evidence together, it was decided that Mrs Creeth was the most likely culprit. Villagers came forward to say that small snippets of gossip that could have been overheard by Mrs Creeth in the post office had subsequently been included in letters to various villagers. The postmistress was duly arrested and sent for trial at Winchester.

The prosecution put up a strong case, but Mrs Creeth was taken ill in the course of the trial and incarcerated in hospital, during which time a letter was posted in Brighstone to her husband, asking him what he intended to do when his wife was in gaol.

The hearing lasted for seven days and the jury retired to consider their verdict. After forty minutes, the foreman announced that they found the defendant not guilty. Mrs Creeth returned home, and from that date there were no more letters, but the drama of the accusation and the trial must have weighed heavy on her for the rest of her days.

Miss Willoughby, the schoolmistress.

Chapter Six

Parkhurst and its Inmates

Parkhurst was never a hanging gaol but, over the years, many men on murder charges found their way behind its bars.

The Reverend Selby Watson – Murderer

Among those listed at the prison in the census of 1881 was John Selby Watson, aged seventy-one, born in Crayford in Kent. His profession was listed as 'Clerk in Holy Orders' and his marital status as 'widower'. Both were significant.

Although his origins seem to have been lowly, as a young man Watson's prospects were good. Having attended Trinity College, Dublin, he was ordained as Deacon to the Bishop of Ely in 1839, and was then ordained priest by the Bishop of Bath and Wells, serving in a Somerset Parish.

Early on, he became engaged to a young Irish woman, Anne Armstrong, but it was a long engagement, Watson being too poor to marry. In 1844, however, he moved to London, taking a post as headmaster of Stockwell Grammar School. The following year, he and Anne were wed.

His time at the school seems to have been fulfilling and he wrote prolifically, producing books, biographies and other pub-

Revd John Selby
Watson breaks the sixth
commandment.

lications, mainly on religious subjects. Then, after twenty-five years' service, the school got into difficulties and, because of falling numbers, they let Watson go, denying him a pension. This was clearly a difficult period for him; he experienced shock at the loss of his job, plus looming poverty.

Perhaps Anne was not the most supportive of wives. Perhaps she was a scold. It has been suggested that she was a drinker. Whatever the case, in October 1871, his servant Ellen Prynne arrived for work to find her master unconscious. She found two letters; one containing her wages and a second addressed to the doctor.

It turned out that Watson had taken prussic acid, but it did not kill him. His letter to the doctor confessed to having murdered Anne, whose body was found in another room, her skull shattered by a heavy object. She had been dead for about two days.

Watson was tried at the Old Bailey. His defence might have been one of provocation, but he chose instead to claim temporary insanity at the time of the act. The jury duly found him guilty but recommended mercy, a plea ignored by the Judge – Mr Justice Byles – who donned his black cap and sentenced him to hang.

There followed an appeal and a flurry of activity, and the Home Office overturned the death sentence, changing it to life in prison. Following on from a plea of insanity, Watson would normally have been consigned to Broadmoor, but he was sent instead to Parkhurst.

Was Watson unfortunate – driven by desperation to commit a crime of violence he then bitterly regretted? Some years later, in an autobiography, F. Vincent Brooks recorded how he had been withdrawn from Stockwell Grammar School following a frenzied beating by Watson, after having been wrongly accused of breaking a window. Brooks concluded that Watson was 'a man of absolutely uncontrollable temper and quite unsuited for a headmaster'. Perhaps Anne Watson had reason to drink, after all.

Watson remained in Parkhurst for twelve years, and on 6 July 1844, he died, following a fall from a hammock. He was buried in Carisbrooke Cemetery.

William Ellison – Police Superintendent and Criminal

After thirty years in the Gloucestershire Police Force, Superintendent William Ellison found himself behind bars.

He was born in the Wiltshire village of Minety, a village that took its name from the plethora of water mint growing in the area. William's father was a tailor by trade. His mother, Catherine, was six years older than her husband, and William was their eldest child. He had one brother, Thomas, two years his junior, and two sisters, Mary and Martha.

In January 1846, William joined the police force. He said that he was twenty years old, making his year of birth 1826. According to the census of 1841, however, he was registered as twelve years old, so he would have been born in 1829. Perhaps like the young recruits in the First World War, he lied to make himself eligible. The following year he married.

William started his police life in Tything Blakeney Parish, Westbury-on-Severn, a Gloucestershire village of about 2,500 residents. It had two schools and a workhouse. By 1851, he and his wife Elizabeth had one daughter, Jane. Ten years later, he had been promoted to the rank of police sergeant and his family had grown from one child to six, Jane having been joined by Henry, William, Mary, Elizabeth and Martha.

Promotion followed again, and by 1871 William was transferred to Chipping Sodbury, a market town in the south of the county. He now held the rank of superintendent. Meanwhile, four more children had made an appearance: Alice, Charles, Sarah Ann and Louisa.

In July 1878, when he would have been fifty-two, William left the police force with an annuity of £80. This was not, however, the honourable retirement (after thirty-two years' service) that it appears to be.

According to the Gloucester Gaol Registers, in February 1879, William Ellison was in prison awaiting trial. The charge: 'Forging several receipts and embezzling five sums of money.' Awaiting trial in the town where he had been an upholder of the law must have been doubly difficult. He was found guilty and sentenced to five years' penal servitude. William was transferred to Parkhurst Prison.

In every way, it was regarded as a tough gaol, and William's sentence came at a time when the powers-that-be were leaning towards harsher treatments for convicts. The inmates worked in silence and when they were not employed on soul-destroying or back-breaking work – picking oakum or breaking rocks – they were locked in single cells. The intention was to ensure that, in the isolation, they contemplated the error of their ways. Food was of the meanest quality, deliberately worse than that of even the poorest person outside of gaol. Flogging was a routine punishment for infringements of the rules. At this time, the uniforms still sported the comic book arrows, while beds were literally made of boards. For William Ellison, one time Police Superintendent, this must have been difficult indeed.

While the children scattered in various directions, Elizabeth and her youngest child Louisa were taken in by a family, the Besleys, who were – like her husband's relatives – tailors. After forty years of marriage, Elizabeth stood by her husband; when he was released, she joined him.

After he completed his sentence, William seems to have been fortunate. Perhaps his crime was regarded as a foolish mistake. The Duke of Beaufort gave him work on his Gloucestershire estate at Badminton, as the lodge keeper. Here, he and Elizabeth seem to have stayed for at least the next ten years, and in their seventies they were found accommodation in the almshouses on the estate. It was there that William died in June 1901.

Richard Kenyon Benham – Swindler

Sometimes, news of a man's actions spread far and wide. In July 1908, the *Otago Witness*, published in New Zealand, reported the death of Richard Kenyon Benham, 'One of the most notorious, unscrupulous and successful swindlers of modern times.' Plausible and ruthless, during his life Benham set up a series of bogus banks and defrauded the public out of thousands of pounds.

In 1880, whilst living at the Buckingham Club at Waterloo Place in London, Benham was declared bankrupt and all his assets sold to repay at least some of his existing debts.

In July 1893, he appeared at the Old Bailey, accused of defrauding the London and General Bank of £40,000. With his younger brother, he was also accused of forging the will of a relative. He was sentenced to fourteen years' imprisonment. In 1901, he was serving his time in Parkhurst.

Among his most celebrated victims was Anthony John Mundella, Liberal MP for Sheffield, who served in Gladstone's government as a member of the Cabinet and, later, President of the Board of Trade. Mundella, who was of Italian origin, campaigned for improvements in education and working conditions for children. He succeeded in getting the hours worked by

children in the textile industry from sixty to fifty-four – still a crippling workload by today's standards.

Mundella's downfall came in 1894. As far as possible, the details were hushed up, but after having been director of the New Zealand Loan Company, the company went into liquidation and Mundella resigned 'in painful circumstances', a victim of Benham's schemes.

Clearly, Benham did not complete his fourteen-year prison sentence, for in 1908, then aged eighty-three, he died 'hungry and penniless' in the flat of a friend in Soho – leaving behind a legacy of misery and ruin for hundreds of people.

Jabez Spencer Balfour – Rogue

Nothing is as satisfying as seeing a scheming criminal get his just desserts. Like a phoenix in reverse, Jabez Balfour rose to the dizzy heights of financial success, before plummeting to earth and spending time in Parkhurst.

Jabez, who was raised in non-conformist piety thanks to his devout mother, who was born on the Isle of Wight, founded the

Liberator Building Society, intended to enable poor people to buy their own homes.

With a flair for making money, he set his eyes on his mother's birthplace and came up with a scheme for draining and extending areas of Brading Marsh. This was a mammoth undertaking that had several times failed in the past, when on each occasion the embankments were washed away by the sea. Undaunted, Balfour tried again and succeeded in establishing a rail link across the marsh to Bembridge and erecting the Royal Spithead Hotel, a prestigious building next to the train station in the fledgling seaside resort.

His financial empire, however, was built on unstable ground. Optimistic forecasts and misleading reports created a false impression, and soon the whole enterprise came toppling down, taking the savings of thousands of little people with it – many of whom, utterly ruined, committed suicide. Jabez fled to Argentina, where he evaded capture for three years but was eventually extradited and sentenced to fourteen years in gaol.

At Parkhurst, Jabez found a cushy number in the library, and at the end of his sentence, although in his seventies, he prepared to go to Burma as a mining engineer. On his return, in a train on the way to Scotland, he entertained fellow passengers with stories of his adventures, then he fell strangely silent. When the train reached its destination, the porter discovered that he had quietly died.

King of the Road

Some men make their own destiny. Irish-born James Phelan grew up on the waterside near Dublin, and the coming and going of the boats, combined with his father's travel stories, made him determined to follow suit.

Faced with a shotgun wedding, he joined an oil tanker and voyaged to America. On his return, he found himself in Liverpool, where he became involved in a series of robberies; then things went dramatically wrong. In 1923, the son of a local postmistress was killed during a raid and Jim was charged with being an accessory to murder. He was sentenced to death. The sentence was then commuted to life in prison and he found himself serving a fifteen-year sentence – much of it in Parkhurst.

It would have been understandable if, being a free spirit and traveller, he would find prison unbearable but, later, he wrote, 'In 1927, I buried myself on the Island and I wrote. I was happy for the jail could deprive me of nothing.'

Although it was prohibited for prisoners to write about prison life, Jim prepared the way for a prolific series of novels, autobiographies, articles and frank accounts of life in Parkhurst. So graphic were some of his descriptions that George Orwell – not normally regarded as squeamish – was moved to say that his description of the sexual lives of prisoners made 'horrible reading, but genuinely horrible', acknowledging that even when locked away, men were still sexual beings.

Sometimes Phelan's work showed the ingenuity of convicts, as in the case of Bill Brummy who succeeded in making a microscope, a telescope and a complete set of chessmen out of illegally acquired pieces of bone and wire. He swapped the chess set with Phelan in exchange for a key.

When he was released, Jim Phelan, again, gave free rein to his wanderlust, travelling the byroads of Britain in the summer and holing up in a caravan and writing about his experiences in the winter. His obvious charisma led him into such unlikely roles as scriptwriter, actor and broadcaster, plus a wide variety of jobs that included navvy, blacksmith, barman, gun runner and tramp. During his travels, he became friendly with Dylan Thomas and was interviewed for the TV programme *Horizon*.

Jim's writings gave a genuine insight into life behind bars in the 1930s. Whereas experts theorised about prison life, Phelan declared, 'I had the men themselves… their chuckles, their groans, their blood and sweat and excrement… jail voices, men sniffing each other from afar…' As Orwell acknowledged, prison life became uncomfortably alive.

Jim died in 1966, leaving in his wake books with such alluring titles as *Nine Murderers and Me*, *Lifer*, and *Jail Journal*.

Crimes Carrying the Death Sentence

Murder, highway robbery, horse theft, house breaking, rape, forgery, sheep stealing, arson and high treason were all crimes that were punishable by death.

Prisoners at Parkhurst were kept busy making hammocks, fenders and nets for the navy, and also coir beds for the army. On the outside, there was always suspicion that work given to the inmates would deprive honest citizens of a living. For this reason, prisoners worked only on government contracts.

Until 1865, new inmates at Parkhurst had to spend the first month sleeping on bare boards without the luxury of a mattress.

Where is he taking Blossom?

Deaths at Parkhurst

1893
20 June: Henry Phillips, aged forty-two, tuberculosis
21 June: William Brooker, aged tweny-four, consumption
26 June: Thomas Whitechurch, fifty-seven, lung and kidney disease

1895
Isaac Foster, aged twenty-one, consumption

1877
24 April: On this day, Mr Thomas Payne, a warder at Parkhurst, was attacked with a hammer by a prisoner who was already in chains following a previous attack. He struck two blows and was restrained by other prisoners, probably saving his life.

1839 – Books Deemed Suitable for Prisoners

Among the books available at Parkhurst were two written on the Island by Revd Legh Richmond, one time curate at Brading. His stories were morally uplifting tales of poor Islanders who had achieved 'goodness' in often short lives. In particular, the books *The Dairyman's Daughter* and *The Young* Cottage were recommended. They were part of a collection entitled *Annals of the Poor*, and this collection has been in print ever since its inception.

Books readily available to prisoners included:

The Holy Bible
The Book of Common Prayer
Broken Catechism
The New Testament
Abridgement of the New Testament
Faith and Duty of a Christian
Chief Tenets of the Christian Religion
Judson's Scripture Questions
Bible Dictionary

Christian Philosophy
Pike's Early Piety
The Sunday Scholars'
Companion (7 volumes)

For light reading:

A History of Quadrupeds
Narrative of Shipwrecks
Readings in Prose
Readings in Poetry
History of the Plague
Robinson Crusoe

For educational purposes:

Spelling
Arithmetic
Easy Lessons in Mechanics
Introduction to Astronomy

'Have you got *The Complete Guide to Tunnelling?*'

Parkhurst was the prison reserved for Jewish prisoners, and for the enlightenment of their Christian fellows, books entitled *Manners and Customs of the Jews* and *Journeys of the Children of Israel*, were also available.

Great Escapes

In 1908, the Governor of Parkhurst Prison stated that there had been no escapes or attempted escapes from Parkhurst for a year, and that the behaviour of the prisoners had been satisfactory.

In spite of this assurance, escapes were, in fact, a regular occurrence. Most escapees were captured within the first twenty-four hours and were usually picked up exhausted and hungry.

In 1922, the escape of Arthur Conmy, serving a sentence for burglary, kept the Islanders reading the latest news for twelve nailbiting days.

Thirty-three-year-old Conmy tunnelled his way out of his cell during the night, placed the removed bricks in his bed so that it appeared to be occupied, then scaled the wall. The warders discovered his absence the next day.

News then reached them that at both Wootton and Havenstreet railway stations, the booking offices had been broken into; a house at Ashey had also been burgled and an amount of food taken.

The following day, a police constable came face-to-face with Conmy, but the elusive prisoner avoided capture and was spotted later by three railwaymen when he ran into woods at Ashey and disappeared.

Another week passed before some of Conmy's prison clothing was discovered under a hedge on the outskirts of Ryde. Meanwhile, the mainland newspapers were having a field day, reporting on the local terror and referring to the Island as the 'Isle of Fright'.

On the twelfth day, Conmy was discovered in the attic of an empty house at George Street, in Ryde. Manacled to two officers, he was escorted to the police station, given a cup of tea and some bread and butter and then transported back to gaol. A large crowd had gathered by the time a car came to collect him, and Conmy was greeted with loud cheers; one lady even presented him with a rose.

Conmy admitted to all the burglaries during his absence, with the exception of those at the two railway stations. He had six months added to his sentence. Later that year, he made another escape but it lasted only a few hours and he was found along the banks of the Medina.

Murderer at Large

The case of Robert Shepherd was altogether more alarming. Serving a prison sentence for murder, he was employed as part of a work gang on a road near to the officers' quarters at Parkhurst in 1922. Suddenly, Shepherd made a bid for freedom, entering the nearby house of prison officer Fry.

Young Ethel Fry was in the process of cleaning the grate when she thought she heard something; opening the door, she found Shepherd in the entrance hall. Before she could react, he grabbed her, and with a piece of rope began to strangle her. Upon hearing the commotion, her mother came to investigate and made a desperate effort to pull the man away from her daughter. In response, he hit Mrs Fry a violent blow on the neck, but she continued the struggle to free Ethel from his grasp. Fortunately for the two women, several prison guards arrived at that moment and Shepherd released them and let the officers in as if nothing untoward had passed. In London, he had murdered a young woman with whom he lived, by tying her up and forcing her to inhale gas through a tube. Ethel must long have lived with the memory of her attack.

The Dartmoor Shepherd Strikes Again

We all have our little foibles, but few would seem stranger than that of David Davies, known as the Dartmoor Shepherd, who could not resist stealing from church poor boxes. In November 1923, at the age of seventy-three, he was released from Parkhurst on licence having spent most of his adult life in prison for robbing churches. In his fifty years behind bars, his sentences had varied from one month's hard labour to fifteen years' penal servitude.

In 1911, he became a *cause célèbre* when he was noticed by Home Secretary Winston Churchill, who was investigating the incidences of re-offending. With David Lloyd George, he visited Davies, who was then at Dartmoor, in charge of the sheep – hence his nickname. He was serving a thirteen-year sentence for stealing a mere 2s. So outrageous did the punishment seem that it was debated in the House of Lords, and Davies was released and provided with employment; almost immediately he re-offended.

His behaviour in prison was always impeccable and, in 1923, when he faced yet another charge of theft, his request to return to his hometown was honoured; he was moved to Llanfyllin Workhouse. A pension was negotiated for him and work provided on a local farm but, once again, he broke out and robbed a local church. In fact, his escapes from the workhouse were so regular that his shoes were confiscated.

In 1929, then nearly eighty years of age, Davies made his last *sortie*, leaving the workhouse and becoming ill whilst at large. His

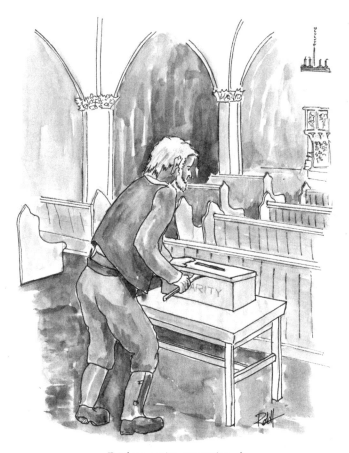

'Lead me not into temptation...'

body was found the following day. He was such a celebrity that local people paid for his funeral.

Poisoning and Painting

Art classes must have been fun at Parkhurst during the 1970s. Whilst notorious East End twins Ronnie and Reggie Kray painted rural landscapes with their initials inscribed on the gateposts of country cottages, poisoner Graham Young worked as a portrait artist, painting the twins for posterity.

Young had been sent to prison convicted of attempted murder by poison, following mysterious family illnesses. His stepmother had already died of poisoning when Young's fascination with toxins brought him to police attention. He was accused of attempting to kill his father, sister and a friend. His stepmother had already been cremated. Young was sentenced to fifteen years in Broadmoor, but after nine years he was deemed to be safe and released.

Thereafter, he found work in a laboratory at Bovington, working on equipment for the army. Some months later, his supervisor died and, over the following weeks, many of his colleagues were taken ill with what was dubbed the Bovington Bug. When Young's past career came to light, he was charged with murder by poisoning his colleagues' tea – and this is how he, Ronnie and Reggie ended up in the same art class.

Whilst in Parkhurst, Young also became good friends with Ian Brady, whose series of child murders horrified the country.

Young confessed to a fear of being poisoned himself, and at the age of forty-two he died in Parkhurst, supposedly from a heart attack, but other theories abounded. Young's portrait of the twins was sold at auction for £3,105.

Still Getting Out?

In recent years, the most celebrated escape happened in 1995 when three prisoners succeeded in making tools, a ladder, a gun, fake ammunition and a key to all the doors – also accumulating £200 in cash – before cutting a hole in the outer fence and absconding. They were at large for three days. Following this debacle, Parkhurst prison was downgraded.

More recently, a murderer serving time at Parkhurst sent out details of his planned escape using lemon juice to create invisible ink. The lemon juice made the ink fade, but it could be reactivated to reveal the ink marks. This was in 2010. The plan was to land a helicopter at the gaol; the instructions were hidden in sodoku code. His plan was discovered though and he was transferred to another prison.

Chapter Seven

Smugglers, Pirates and the Sea

The Island's Oldest Profession?

If numbers of murder incidences on the Isle of Wight were always far down the national league table, when it came to smuggling,

Something for all the family.

the Island was in the Premier League. For centuries, Island people made their livings from the sea, by both legal and illegal means.

In 1822, the press reported that the state of contraband traffic on the Island coast was greater than at any time they could remember, and there was systematic smuggling from St Helens to Yarmouth. The reason for it continuing was that goods which might be bought abroad for 6 or 7d (37½ pence) could be sold at home for more than £2, which meant there was no reason to expect the trade to decrease.

Pinching the Monks' Wine

One early, high profile prosecution for stealing the cargo of a wrecked ship saw Walter de Godeton, the Lord of Chale, on trial in Southampton. The charge was stealing wine from the French ship *St Marie de Bayonne*, which was wrecked in Chale Bay on 20 April 1313. The *St Marie* carried white wine headed for the monastery of Livers in Picardy, so de Godeton was also tried by the church court and threatened with excommunication.

His penance was to build a lighthouse above the site of the wreck on St Catherine's Down. He was also to erect an oratory and to pay for a priest to tend the light and to say Mass for the souls of the drowned. The lighthouse, known locally as the Pepper Pot, was maintained until the Reformation. In terms of effectiveness, it was rarely useful; it was often swathed in fog.

Those French monks will be furious!

Woolly Jumpers

In 1394, Thomas Symode, the rector of All Saints' – the Saxon parish church at Freshwater – was accused of smuggling woollen cloth. This local, rather rough cloth, known as Kersey, had incurred a tax and was, therefore, worth smuggling abroad. Symonde was caught red-handed but claimed 'benefit of clergy', by which a minister of the church could not be tried by a secular law. At some point, a wag recorded the event in verse, beginning, 'Ye Rector of Freshwater, Was dogg'd and collared at Ye Red Lion Inne. A matter of conflict betwixte Church and State, He was snuggled, in smuggled woolle next Ye Skinne…'

Changing the Law

In the eighteenth century, a highly successful smuggler, David Boyce, was living at Ryde. With his ill-gotten gains, he built himself an impressive mansion facing the sea at Ryde, known as Appley House. Every attempt to bring a successful prosecution against him failed; it was common knowledge that he bribed the sheriff and the jury with his wealth and reputation.

In 1773, he unknowingly caused an important change in the law, when an act was introduced making it compulsory to store the names of all potential jurors in a locked box, from which they were to be drawn at random. As a result, Boyce was convicted of smuggling and died at Fleet Prison in 1740. His grand house at Appley is now home to Benedictine nuns and is known as St Cecilia's Abbey.

The Back of the Wight

At its height, two thirds of Island sailors and fishermen were confidently reckoned to be involved in smuggling.

The main theatre of operations was along the south coast of the Island, known locally as the 'Back of the Wight', but in fact activity was everywhere. One of the main centres of distribution was at Rookley, pretty well in the centre, thus making it a useful halfway point for moving goods around. Certainly the Island was dealing with the problem of smuggling by 1575, when a customs house was established at Cowes.

The scale of the ongoing problem is highlighted by the number of prosecutions reported in the press. On 16 February 1830, the *Hampshire Telegraph* carried reports on the following prosecutions: Israel Rolf of Gatcombe, Henry Rolf of Chillerton, Daniel Scamel of Wellow, James Gallop of Mottistone, Simon Singleton of Whitwell, and William Warne of Atherfield. They were all charged with having various amounts of illegal spirits in their possession, and were each fined the sum of £25.

On 25 February, the *Telegraph* recorded that Mary Sweatman of Ryde and John Stagg of Calbourne were convicted of having contraband liquor in their possession. Mary was fined £50 and James £25.

A Fair Cop

While smugglers might have accepted prosecution as an occupational hazard, in terms of time and profit, it cost them dearly. Acts of violence or intimidation, particularly against the excise men, often occurred. Once a smuggler was 'wanted' it was a brave local who would come forward with evidence against him.

In 1716, Richard Young was employed as mate on the customs yacht *Greenhill*, patrolling the Island's coast. The crew's brief was to report anything suspicious to the customs officers. Encountering a suspect ship, a confrontation followed, during which Young was killed. His attacker was William Harris, who fled the scene. A description was circulated but there is no evidence that Harris was caught.

In July 1804, a £50 reward was offered for the apprehension of three men who had bludgeoned customs men Daniel Dore and George Grainger. Having seized forty casks of spirits, the two officers temporarily stored them at Bembridge but before they could remove them to the customs house at Cowes, the felons broke in and stole them back, attacking the officers in the process.

Captain Miller Worsley was employed by the revenue service as Inspector of Preventive Boats, joining the service after a distinguished career in the navy. He was present at Trafalgar and served in Canada during the Anglo-American war of 1812. February 1819 was a month filled with incident. Riding on his way from inspecting the revenue boats on 8 February, he met a runaway wagon in a narrow lane and, being unable to get out of the way in time, was thrown from his horse. He was taken to the house of his brother, Revd Henry Worsley, at Godshill, where he made a recovery; the horse died in the accident. On 25 February, he was 'feloniously fired upon' by an unknown person from a copse near Wroxall. An award of £100 was offered for the perpetrator's capture.

William Robey and Robert Lyall, two officers, surprised a gang of smugglers, causing them to abandon their haul of brandy. They were then fired on near Ryde. A reward of £100 was offered for the miscreants' apprehension.

There was a nasty attack at Totland Bay when a customs man was stoned to death when he confronted a crew landing a smuggled cargo. Perhaps even worse, at Alum Bay, a brave but foolish officer tried to prevent a craft from taking to the sea by hanging on to the stern. He was threatened with violence but refused to let go; a crewman then struck him with a bill-hook, severing his hands.

Sometimes an injury was accidental. Following a fall at Chine Avenue, Shanklin, a coastguard, suffered serious injuries. In falling, he landed on his pistol, which then went off. The shot 'completely misplaced his heart' and drove 'one lung into a small lump'. Not surprisingly, the poor man died three days later. He was buried at Brading.

Sometimes the customs men were the perpetrators. In the churchyard at Binstead stands a memorial to sixty-four-year-old Thomas Sivell, who died on 15 June 1785 when he was mistaken for a smuggler and shot. In fact, he was innocently plying his trade in the Solent. His tombstone, erected by his distraught wife, carried a warning:

> All you that pass, pray look and see;
> How soon my life was took from me;
> By those officers as you hear;
> They spill'd my blood that was so dear;
> But God is Good is Just and True,
> And will reward to each their due.

Smuggling as a Sideline

In 1870, James Spanner, dairyman and market gardener had in his possession six bottles of smuggled brandy, plus other liquors, that had landed at Chale. He appeared at the court petty sessions and although he admitted guilt, he denied all knowledge of a cask in his possession; he said it was found in a field next to his house. He was fined £5 10s with £2 costs.

Similarly, George Cooper, grocer and butcher, was charged with having foreign-manufactured tobacco in his possession, while Mr James, baker of Carisbrooke, was found guilty of conveying contraband liquor and fined £100.

Newspapers routinely carried reports of smuggling prosecutions. *The Salisbury and Winchester Journal* of March 1825 recorded that a seaman, referred to only as Midlane, was accused of assaulting and obstructing William Adams the younger, a police constable in the execution of his duty. Midlane went to the rescue of Charles Bright, newly arrested for a smuggling transaction, and freed him from Constable Adams' custody. A warrant had been issued for the arrest of Bright some weeks before, but he had disappeared. Then, as Adams was travelling on his father's cart, he espied Bright along with Midlane and another man. Immediately, he grabbed him by the collar and Bright offered him £5 to let him go. When Adams refused, Midlane crept up behind him and pinioned his arms, shouting 'Run Charlie!' to Bright, who made his escape. He had not been seen since. Several witnesses confirmed the events and Midlane was found guilty; he was sentenced to twelve months in prison. The judge told him that had he not produced a young witness who attempted to perjure himself, his sentence would have been halved. The same paper reported that much of the court's time on 1 July 1825 was taken up with revenue issues.

George Lewis, a local butcher, had been arrested for possession of a quantity of illegal brandy. He protested, saying that he had bought it from a local dealer and had the receipt to prove it. Not convinced, the officers had it tested and it was found to be of a dark variety not sold locally. Mr Lewis was fined £50 – no small amount – which he promptly paid up.

At the same hearing, William Woodnut of Carisbrooke, Robert Sparke of Chale, and James Blow of Newport were all convicted of similar offences.

The Customs Officer

In 1777, William Arnold, father of Thomas Arnold of Rugby School fame, was appointed Collector of Customs for the Island, based at East Cowes. At the time, it was reported: 'Smugglers, in general, are becoming more daring than ever, and more frequently assemble in numbers, carrying arms and in disguise. Instances occur every year of officers being wounded, beaten, opposed and obstructed in the execution of their duty…'

Customs officers augmented their salaries by receiving a share of the profits from selling off contraband goods. Being the time of war (with the United States), many privateers were active, slipping close to the shore at night to be met with as many as 300 smugglers ready to carry off up to a thousand casks of brandy

Many local people were sympathetic to the smugglers and would lend a hand in an emergency. A house with a ship carved into the stone indicated that a smuggler could call on help within.

Customs Prosecutions 1751–1829

Unless violence was involved, prosecutions for smuggling usually resulted in the confiscation of goods and a fine of three times their value. If the accused then failed to pay the fine, he or she would be sent to gaol.

If the smuggler had a boat, that vessel was invariably seized along with its cargo and sold.

Any smuggler who was a seaman might be sentenced to five years and handed over to the navy to serve his time aboard one of their vessels. The most common destination was HMS *Victory*. Those subsequently found unfit to serve were sent instead to gaol.

When found guilty of a felony and given a financial penalty, the felon often had the choice of whether to pay up or go to gaol. An alternative might be to give information that would lead to further prosecutions.

The charges brought in court included running goods, harbouring or concealing, receiving goods, obstructing an officer in the course of his duty, smuggling, signalling illegally, having goods in the house, and being found aboard a ship carrying contraband.

Some examples of charges brought and sentences imposed: John Fleming for carrying an anker [*sic*] of gin aboard his wherry, for which his boat was seized; Thomas Price the elder, with others, for running goods. He was sent to Winchester Gaol but the prosecution was stopped, in consideration of information given; John Boss and others for throwing casks overboard a vessel. They were sentenced to serve in the navy.

In 1821, James Gillman of Whippingham was charged with having in his custody candles, apples, a basket, tea, and butter, knowing the same to be landed without payment of duty. Perhaps the customs man had been overzealous and the magistrates charged him only with the possession of the candles. The cost for the candles was £3.

On 22 July of the same year, at Hants Assizes, William Stone and Stephen Day were accused of making a fire to signal to people a smuggling boat. Day received two months and Stone one month in Newport Gaol.

In 1826, both James Whitewood and Abraham Redstone were convicted of having smuggled tea in their possession. The original fines of £100 each were mitigated to £25.

In December 1826, James Rayner of Freshwater was arrested for having fifty casks of foreign spirits in his custody, twenty-one bags of tea and one cask of foreign wine. He was charged a penalty of three times the value of the stolen goods. However, presumably Rayner did not pay up, as he was then committed to Winchester Gaol.

John Saunders was found guilty of having a quantity of foreign geneva (gin) concealed on his person. In default of payment, he went to prison.

John Hayles, a baker from Nettlestone, was charged with making signals to smugglers. Found guilty, he served four months' hard labour in the House of Correction.

Jacob Wells and several men found illegally on board his ship, *The Jacob Wells*, were impressed into the navy. Similarly, three men illegally aboard the ship *Albion* were taken to serve at sea.

In December 1825, William Cawes, John Calloway, William Serle and Nicholas Moorman were all charged with being on the high seas with eighty-eight tubs of foreign brandy – the first two went to the navy; the second two defaulted on payment and were sent to prison, as they were unfit for naval service.

The prosecutors occasionally gave the accused the benefit of the doubt, as in the case of Daniel Brading of Northwood, who was acquitted on the charge of carrying and conveying ninety casks of foreign spirits. His claim was that he had seen the casks accidentally and was actually conveying them to the customs house when he was apprehended.

Similarly, John Webster of Yarmouth was acquitted when it was decided that he did not know that he was carrying 3 quarts of smuggled, foreign gin. His initial sentence had been impressment into the navy.

While smuggling was synonymous with brandy and tobacco, from an early age, one of the Island's main preoccupations was with salt.

Pass the Salt

For some 800 years, salt was processed around the Island coast, particularly at Newtown and Seaview. The names 'Salterns' and 'Saltings' remain as a reminder.

To extract salt, seawater was stored in collecting ponds to dry out during the summer months, and then boiled in huge pans to form crystals. The industry was particularly hit by a salt tax introduced in 1693, and smuggling salt became rife, as evidenced by the list of salt officers employed on the Island during the eighteenth century. They were variously known as Officer of Salt Duty, salt officer, salt watchman, and Officer of Excise and Salt.

Salt officers were based in the following locations: Shalfleet, Newtown and Thorley, Elmsworth (East of Newtown), Cowes, Freshwater, Nettlestone, Calbourne, and Thorness.

The smuggling trade ceased when the salt tax was finally removed in 1824. Many more customs officers were involved in patrolling the coast, collecting excise duty, seizing

Chips never taste the same without it.

contraband goods and prosecuting smugglers. Inadvertently, the smugglers had spawned a job creation scheme.

The Revenue Men

One of the perks, or perhaps one should say 'incentives', for the revenue men was the receipt of a percentage of the value of goods taken by individual officers. In November 1822, it was reported that following a seizure of goods at the premises of James Rayner in the Parish of Godshill, the arresting officers wished to bear the cost of arresting Rayner themselves, in expectation that they would receive one third of the penalty for the recovered goods.

Contraband seized was often put up for sale and advertised in newspapers. On 22 February 1802, forty-six half barrels of Red Herrings were auctioned at the East Cowes customs house, while a fully equipped boat, known as the *Resolution*, was offered for sale at the Fountain Hotel, West Cowes in February 1800.

In July 1801, a condemned lot of un-manufactured tobacco, short cut tobacco, shag tobacco, and Scotch snuff – totalling 1,897 lbs in weight – went under the hammer at East Cowes. Literally, thousands of barrels of brandy were seized.

Things did not always go to plan. On 10 June 1869, the *Isle of Wight Times* reported the appearance of George Colenut at the County Court, on charges of smuggling ashore 125 gallons of spirits and of being illegally aboard a certain vessel on the night in question. The coastguard had witnessed the boat landing between one and two in the morning, and a total of forty-two tubs were later found on the beach near Luccombe Chine. The boat contained some rope that was similar to that wrapped around the tubs. As this was the only evidence – and in reference to the fact that Colenut was a fisherman and therefore likely to be at sea and to carry rope – the magistrates took no time in dismissing the case.

Royal Shenanigans

In August 1852, Queen Victoria must have been outraged to learn that, following her visit to Antwerp with a flotilla of her escorts – known as the Royal Squadron – an inspection by customs officers revealed widespread smuggling of tobacco. The felony came to light when an Antwerp newspaper, the *Journal de Commerce*, reported on the benefits of the royal visit, where some 5,000lbs of tobacco had been purchased from local shops. A total of 80lbs of the contraband were found on the royal yacht *Victoria and Albert*, and four of the crew from the squadron were later found in possession of illegal tobacco. They were Samuel White, William Long, Robert Layton and George Cox. The tobacco was purchased for 4d per lb in Antwerp and had a market value of 3/6d a lb in England.

It seems that the royal yacht *Victoria and Albert* long remained under suspicion and customs kept an eye on her for decades. They were finally rewarded the Queen's Golden Jubilee Year in 1887, when the yacht was lying in Cowes Road while Her Majesty took a holiday at Osborne. Deciding on a night out, some of the crew set out for Portsmouth but were stopped and searched by Cowes customs men. This resulted in a haul of 40lbs of cigars and tobacco. The seven crewmembers were collected by the yacht's captain, Fullerton, and held on board to await trial. How Queen Victoria must have suffered!

Hauls were picked up in all parts of the Island, from Yaverland to Luccombe, St Helens to Shanklin, Chale to Compton. They were also found in unlikely places, weighted, and tied to lobster pots at sea – in coves and caves around the shore, in cellars, pigsties, hedges and even graves.

Mark Norman, an Islander who wrote a journal of his life, confirmed that nearly everyone living at Niton was involved – in some way – in smuggling brandy from France. Mark, a radical campaigner for political reform, was the Island's representative for the planned launch of a national newspaper *Friend of the People* in 1851.

Lifeboat Men: Heroes and Villains?

Not surprisingly, those men who made their living from the sea and supplemented their income by smuggling were also the first to volunteer for the lifeboats. Records tell of brave attempts to rescue shipwrecked mariners – some local fishermen losing their lives in the attempt. These same men, however, often supplemented their incomes with a haul of smuggled liquor.

In March 1878, sailing from France with a ship loaded with barrels of brandy, the lifeboat-man, Rufus Cotton, and his crew came upon the wreck of the *Eurydice*, the training ship carrying 300 men – mostly young cadets. Within sight of land, a sudden squall had capsized her. Most of those on board were trapped and only two ultimately survived. Cotton and his crew came upon the scene but were unable to help because every available space on their craft was filled with illegal barrels. Later, they must have pondered if they might not have saved lives by sacrificing their cargo.

James Snudden, Customs Officer

The revenue men, the coast and tide waiters, and the riding officers who lived in the midst of fishing communities were often objects of mistrust and hate. Meanwhile, they kept the courts busy with prosecutions. The life of James Snudden, local man and riding officer, illustrates their difficulties.

James Snudden was an Island man, born and baptised in 1778 at Brook. In 1891, he was accepted as a coast waiter – an onshore customs officer whose job it was to bring smugglers to court – at Newport. At first glance, it must have seemed a secure employment but men were not queuing up for the jobs. In James' case it was enough that 'he was of fair character'. He had not been convicted of smuggling and was not known to have obstructed revenue officers in the course of their duty. If the requirements for the job sound minimal, he was soon to find out why.

In 1804, a £100 reward was offered for the capture of three unknown men who had attacked James Snudden while he was protecting a cart on the way to the customs house at Cowes.

James Snudden always gets his man!

The cart contained fifteen casks of prohibited spirit. The felons had lain in wait along the route and set about him with cudgels making away with five of the casks.

This was the beginning of James' troubles. A few years into his service, his inability to handle his finances, and the failure of the customs service to pay its bills on time, landed him in serious trouble. One can only speculate as to the sort of man he was, but his honesty and courage were never questioned.

One of the conditions of service was that officers initially undertook to cover costs involving their work, to be repaid in due course. In January 1807, James submitted a bill for £8 19s 6d, for expenses incurred in the shipping and landing of corn and flour at a distance from his station.

As an incentive, officers were paid a proportion of the goods they seized. First they had to be sold, and this took some time. In 1810, James was appealing to the authorities to consider the loss he had sustained over the sale of Peruvian Bark. At the time of its confiscation, the bark was a rare medicinal item and it was confidently expected to sell for up to 30s per lb. The haul was of 100lbs, thus promising James a moiety of £75. It was not sold immediately, however, and in the meantime, more bark had been imported so that the value per pound dropped, dramatically, to 6s. Clearly, James had already spent the money in expectation of the

£75. Now he asked for these peculiar circumstances to be taken into consideration.

James married, and with his wife Hannah produced eight children – a considerable family to support. In June 1810, he was sent to work at Ryde where the current officer, Mr Chiverton, was suffering from early signs of insanity. After one month, Mr Chiverton returned to work and James submitted a bill for £36 15s for costs incurred in having to live away from home. Things gradually grew more serious.

In March 1814, James was forced to take leave of absence. The reason was stark – he was consigned to the county gaol in Newport because he could not pay his debts. In April, he requested an extension of leave and the authorities were forced to find a replacement officer to take over his duties. It says something about his character, however, that there was no decision to dismiss him from the service.

At the end of June, another request to extend his leave of absence was made. James was confident that by the end of this time, his difficulties would be resolved. His case was put before the Court of Relief of Insolvent Debtors, and anyone owed money by him was asked to come forward. The list of creditors amounted to about forty individuals. Those to whom he owed money were as varied as a hosier, a surgeon, an upholsterer, the butcher and grocer, moneylenders, and a tutor for his children. Once the case was settled, James returned to work.

He went first to Shanklin and then to Niton – his post at Newport had been filled. In 1815, he was appointed riding officer and his work was exemplary. Between 1815 and 1818, his seizures included a two-oared boat and 337 casks of illicit spirits, plus the apprehension of several smugglers.

In the meantime, James, once again, faced mounting debts. A year after his appointment as riding officer, he was still awaiting confirmation of his post, and the proposal to make him riding officer first class had not been honoured three years later.

By January 1818, James was begging the board to pay him his entitlement of Seizure Awards, amounting to £32 13s 10d, declaring that he was in 'distressed circumstances'.

On 11 January 1822, he captured James Dore and John Stocks in the act of plundering a wreck. Shortly afterwards, written threats were issued against his life and he wrote requesting that a reward should be offered to catch the authors. He must have felt in a very vulnerable position.

Later that year, aged only thirty-nine, James died after a short illness. His wife Hannah, faced with destitution, threw herself on the mercy of the Director of the Customs Fund. James left his wife a legacy of poverty, and in the 'List of Paupers' of 1834 in the Parish of Newchurch, there was Hannah Snudden, now sixty-three years of age and in need of help to pay her rent. A customs officer's lot was not a happy one.

Caves and Caverns

It was essential to hide contraband as soon as possible, and it found its way into all manner of places – under hedgerows, in cellars, pig sties, under wood piles, even in church vaults and graves. Caves thereby provided an ideal solution. The following caves were employed for this purpose:

At Bonchurch – Old Jack

At Brighstone – Dutchman's Hole

Below Tennyson Down/Freshwater Cliffs – Frenchman's Hole, so named because a Frenchman hiding in the cave was rumoured to have starved to death; cave is listed as 90ft deep

Neptune Caves – one some 200ft deep the other 90ft

Bat Cave – 90ft deep

Lord Holmes' Parlour – named for Sir Robert Holmes, who allegedly entertained friends in the cave

Lord Holmes' Kitchen – where Sir Robert reportedly stored his wine

Roe Hall – apparently 600ft high

Luccombe Beach – a natural cave in the cliff, probably since lost in landslides

Undercliff Cave – featured in a painting by Edward William Coke, 1836

Watcombe Bay Cave – in the chalk cliffs near the Needles, rated 69th of the world's longest sea cave

Culver Cliff – called 'the Nostrils'

Along the Undercliff – known locally as Elephant Hole

Keep Your Head Down

Rudyard Kipling may well have had the Island in mind when he wrote his poem, 'A Smuggler's Song'. The opening lines convey a sense of the dangerous world of smuggling:

If you wake at midnight, and hear a horse's feet,
Don't go drawing back the blind, or looking in the street…

Chapter Eight

The Ones that Got Away

The Island Governor Falls Foul of the Law

The swashbuckling, larger-than-life career of Sir Robert Holmes, the Island's Governor, was never without incident. Born in Ireland and serving King Charles I during the Civil War, following the Royalist defeat he embarked on a piratical world tour with the King's nephews Prince Rupert and Prince Maurice. During their adventures, Prince Maurice met an unfortunate end; he probably drowned in the Caribbean, although rumours of his being taken into slavery persisted. Thereafter, Holmes was mostly at sea, and he is credited with starting not one, but two wars against the Dutch.

In 1660, he held the post of Captain of Sandown Castle. It was to the Island that he retired from military service eight years later, where he became Governor of the Isle of Wight.

In 1665, he found himself facing a death sentence for the murder of Sir John Jenkins. The trouble arose when George, the 2nd Duke of Buckingham, took as his mistress Anna Maria Talbot, the wife of the Earl of Shrewsbury. Humiliated, Shrewsbury challenged Buckingham to a duel. Both men appointed two seconds and in the custom of the time, all six individuals took part in the event. The Duke of Buckingham had as his accomplices Sir John

Anybody good at carving heads?

Jenkins and Sir Robert Holmes, while Shrewsbury was assisted by Sir John Talbot, a relative and Lord Bernard Hopkins.

The resultant skirmish was something of a bloodbath. The Earl was run through with a sword, piercing his right breast and causing a wound from which he died two months later. His kinsman, Sir John, suffered serious wounds to both arms and Sir John Jenkins was mortally wounded, dying at the scene. The Duke of Buckingham had minor injuries and Holmes escaped unscathed.

The event was gleefully recorded by Samuel Pepys, who had reason to both dislike and fear Holme – the latter having paid considerable attention to his wife, Elizabeth. He also despised Buckingham, condemning him as being a man of 'no more sobriety than to fight about a whore'. A legend circulated that the object of the dispute came in disguise to watch the fighting, holding Buckingham's horse.

The survivors faced execution for murder. This posed a problem for King Charles II, who had a fondness for Buckingham. In spite of initial royal intervention on the duellists' behalf, in February Holmes found himself charged with murder at Surrey Assizes. The King then hastily issued a warrant, granting him and the others a reprieve, a step too far that brought down disapproval on the royal house.

Rumour circulated that Holmes had been involved in another duel with his arch naval rival, Sir Jeremy Smith, with whom he had quarrelled over the conduct of the St James' Day naval battle against the Dutch. The St James' Day Fair is still celebrated at Yarmouth.

In spite of these controversies, Holmes maintained his position as Governor, acquiring much of the West Wight and building himself a house in the grounds of Yarmouth Castle (now the George Hotel), plus a manor house at Thorley for his only acknowledged child, Mary. He died on 18 November 1891, and was buried with some pomp in Yarmouth church. The statue in his chapel is said to have started life as a monument to King Louis XIV, but having been captured, Holmes had the head carved in his own image.

Diplomatic Dilemma

From Victorian times, the organ grinder was a familiar part of the Island's summer entertainment. On 8 August 1901, however, Venquinze Rea, an Italian organ grinder, was found shot dead. The perpetrator was believed to be a fellow itinerant, Raffieli de Cicco, but by the time a search was instigated, de Cicco had fled the country and made his way to the United States.

There followed a long, drawn-out debate as to how to get him back. There were diplomatic considerations, and it took until 1906 for the Home Office to consider whether to ask the Italian Government to request his extradition on behalf of the British. Upon reflection, they decided against this plan, for it would give the Italians the opportunity to deal the government a humiliat-

ing rebuff. The Home Office spokesman explained that, as the United States Government was always reluctant to part with any criminals, perhaps it would be wiser just to let them keep Signor de Cicco after all.

Get Outta Town!

In September 1860, when the summer season was at an end, Italian entertainer Lazarus Manuel accused police constable 171 John Kingshot of assault – and he had the bruises to prove it. The trouble started because Kingshot had already told him to get out of Ventnor – the reason being that Manuel, along with his performing 'learned' dog and his monkey, had frightened several women by 'intruding himself' into their houses. According to Kingshot, when he approached Manuel, the Italian had set his dog and his monkey onto him, and in the ensuing punch up it was Manuel who came off worst. After hearing the evidence, the court decided

that as Manuel had started the incident, their advice to him was to leave the Island as soon as possible. Kingshot joined the force at West Cowes in 1869, serving first on the Island and then at Liphook in Hampshire. Unlike his brother George, who became Superintendent of Police for Hampshire, John was content to remain a constable until his retirement twenty-five years later.

Why Spelling is Important

Playwright and priest Nicholas Udall served as vicar of All Saints' at Calbourne for three years. He possibly lost his position for religious reasons when Catholic Queen Mary I came to the throne. Previously, he had been headmaster of Eton College – a 'poorly paid but honourable post', where he had a reputation as a 'flogger'. During this time, he was accused of stealing school plate and also of buggery (a capital offence), for which he was committed to Marshalsea Prison. His defenders insisted that the charge was a 'clerical error', and that the word should have been 'burglary'. He later came under the patronage of Queen Catherine Parr and presented various pageants at court. His lasting drama was a play, *Ralph Roister Doister*, recognised as the first English comedy. He died in 1556.

Foul Deeds

There was, no doubt, a hushed shock in the servants' hall at Steephill Castle on 10 August 1893, when it was learned that Cecil Hambrough, twenty-year-old son, heir of their master, Dudley Hambrough, had met with a fatal accident.

The maids may have sobbed but the older, wiser employees would have shaken their heads knowingly and whispered that they had always feared the boy would meet a bad end.

At the time of his death, young Cecil was up in Scotland for the shooting season. It seemed that he had got up early and gone for a walk. He tripped over a wall and his gun went off.

Cecil had long been causing his father, Dudley, sleepless nights. He was wild and a spendthrift; Cecil had a gift for getting into bad company, and in desperation his father hired a tutor to try and divert him from his errant ways. Soon he would reach his twenty-first birthday and become independent, and he was heir to an inheritance from the Hambrough banking business, estimated to be worth £250,000.

An inquest was held and a verdict of accidental death declared. Cecil's body was returned to Ventnor for burial. It was accompanied by his sorrowing tutor, thirty-three-year-old Alfred Motson.

Dudley would have started the process of mourning for his son, but a sudden revelation stunned the family. Six days before Cecil's death, Motson had taken out a life insurance policy on his pupil in the name of Motson's wife – for £20,000. The case was re-opened and the body ordered to be exhumed.

Dudley insisted on being present, and on 13 September, Cecil was disinterred and examined. The pathologist pronounced that the shot that had killed him had been fired from at least 9ft away and that it came from Motson's gun.

Alfred Motson was arrested and put on trial. It was revealed that, in spite of being heavily in debt, Motson had persuaded Cecil that they should jointly lease the Ardlamont House estate in Scotland for the grouse season. Cecil had no money but because he was shortly to inherit his fortune, Motson took out the life insurance on him as protection in case Cecil did not reach his majority. If he died before that date, £20,000 would go to his tutor's wife.

Although being pursued by creditors, at the time Motson employed a butler, coachman and a tutor for his children. When renting the estate, he even arranged the services of a steam yacht so that the party could tour around the loch at their leisure.

Only the day before the shooting, Cecil had nearly drowned when a boat in which he and Motson were sailing capsized. Cecil could not swim, but

Cecil Hambrough;
a young man about town.

managed to hold on to a rock until he was rescued.

It seemed like an open-and-shut case. Motson swore that it was he who had rescued Cecil from the loch so he was certainly unlikely to have tried to kill him. Other details emerged about Motson's association with questionable characters but, against all the odds, the jury were not totally convinced of his guilt and brought in that peculiarly Scottish verdict of 'not proven'.

The blow to the Hambroughs must have been great. Three years later, Motson did end up in gaol for insurance fraud and for failing to support his now abandoned wife and children.

After the sad loss of their son, every year, on the anniversary of his death, the Hambroughs inserted an 'In Memoriam' in the *Glasgow Herald* with the words, 'Vengeance is Mine: I will repay, saith the Lord.'

Smelling of Roses?

On 17 February 1892, the funeral of James Binfield Bird of Cowes took place with all the pomp one could wish for. Along the route, curtains were drawn, flags flew at half-mast and the road from Cowes to Northwood Cemetery was lined with mourners. Anyone who was anyone sent floral tributes, including violet hearts from the widow and bereaved children, while Miss Hookey, who had been the dead man's nanny, sent a floral anchor. There were wreaths from the Dean of Westminster, Admiral de Horsey, Sir Godfrey Baring, members of the Seely family and Inspector McGlaughlan, who kept the crowd in order. Sixty members of the Court Foresters Isle wore black scarves and carried laurel leaves.

The *County Press* reported that at the graveside, the mourners took one last look 'at the remains of him whom everybody liked'. But he was not universal popular; the Ward family of Northwood House, at Cowes, certainly did not like him and as his virtues were extolled, Bird would not have wished mourners to dwell too long on certain aspects of his past.

Even as the funeral took place, his former associate, Jabez Balfour, was languishing in Parkhurst Prison, accused of embezzlement. Bird had been involved up to his neck in the scandal that saw Balfour consigned to gaol.

For sixteen years, Bird had been agent to the Ward family but around 1875, unease crept in as to his trustworthiness. The Wards initiated an enquiry and the result was a dispute over the ownership of carriages, horses, and even an iron safe. Mr Bird was asked to vacate the premises.

Fortunately for him, that year the Brading Harbour scheme got under way and he found employment. Later, it was to come back to haunt him. The scheme to drain Brading Harbour was an ambitious one, and when questions were first asked as to the finances of Balfour's empire, Jabez was forced to agree to an independent enquiry carried out by the respectable London firm Driver & Co. Their findings confirmed suspicions that the Corporation's assets were grossly over-valued.

Fortunately for Jabez Balfour, Mr Driver had in his employ a certain James Binfield Bird, who agreed to inform his employer that the report on Balfour was no longer needed. Mr Driver took his fee and thought no more about it.

Bird was now employed to present his own report, his findings being quite the opposite from those of Mr Driver. Balfour assured his creditors that a more capable, straightforward or honest man than Bird did not exist, Bird's version of the situation was accepted and he was awarded a seat on the board of the Lands Allotment Company.

Quite how he avoided being tarnished when the deception was discovered is difficult to believe but as his obituary shows, James Binfield Bird became a pillar of Cowes society.

The Law is an Ass

On 6 March 1878, in a freak squall, the training ship *Eurydice* inexplicably sank off Dunnose Point, with the loss of 330 lives. The ship *Emma*, captained by Langworthy Jenkins, was in the vicinity and managed to pick up five men but of those, only two survived. They were Able Seaman Benjamin Cuddiford and Ordinary Seaman Sidney Fletcher. After an enquiry, although they were only ordinary crewmembers, the pair were then court-martialled, accused of losing their ship. At the same time, the captain of the *Emma* was severely criticised for failing to revive the other three rescued men because, being a temperance ship, he had no brandy on board with which to revive them. Happily for Cuddiford and Fletcher, they were acquitted.

At the Old Bailey, 21 August 1848

In very sad circumstances, Mrs Mary Ann Dore stood accused of the murder of her daughter Mary Ann Theresa.

On 13 July 1848, a young mother, Mary Ann Dore, living in London, where her husband was in service, was invited to make a visit to the Isle of Wight by her mother's friend Mrs Merton. The outing was intended as a treat and the two women travelled by train, Mrs Merton first class and Mary Ann electing to travel second class, to save her benefactor the expense. Mary Ann had her four-month-old daughter, Mary Ann Theresa, with her; the baby had been taken ill overnight. In fact, so unwell had she become that Mary Ann had sent for a surgeon to prescribe some medicine and to confirm whether the little one was fit to travel.

Mr Woolmer, the local surgeon and general practitioner, was away and his practice was left in the hands of Mr Driver, who, in turn, left his assistant, Frederick Hustler, to oversee things and to summon Mr Driver if necessary.

The baby was believed to be teething and Mr Hustler felt that her condition did not merit sending for Mr Driver, so he dispensed a draft of calcined magnesia, aniseed water and syrup of poppies. It came in a phial containing eight doses of one teaspoon each. He also prescribed a powder of calomel and sugar, a small proportion to be given at night. He told Mrs Dore that the child was well enough to travel.

During the journey, the baby became increasingly distressed. By the time they reached Ryde, her condition was such that the landlady of Stamford House, Mrs Stamp, recommended a local surgeon called Mr Bloxham.

When Mr Bolxham came, he diagnosed colic and lanced the baby's swollen gums. He told her mother to give her a warm bath and prescribed a 'grey' powder – a mixture of mercury and chalk. He also sent round castor oil to be taken an hour after the powder. By next morning, he was summoned again and by now, baby Mary was clearly very ill and he suspected intussusception – a bowel condition. He gave the baby a saline mixture of carbonate of soda and citric acid.

Horatio Thomas Watermouth, Bloxham's assistant, was later to give evidence that, as directed, he had dispensed two grains of quicksilver, one ounce of castor oil and a saline mixture composed of a scruple of sesquicarbonate of soda and about fifteen grains of citric acid.

Mary Ann's mother was in such distress that, suspecting that the child was dying, Bloxham agreed that she should return to London.

By the time they reached the capital, the baby was vomiting and her nappies were stained with blood. Mr Driver was now summoned, and he ordered a dose of castor oil to be given at intervals and a mustard poultice to be applied to the stomach. Two hours later, there was no improvement and shortly afterwards Mary Ann Theresa died.

Her mother was in a state of shock but her grandmother was clearly suspicious as to the circumstances of the baby's death. There was, however, a suggestion that the child might have been fed something other than the medication properly prescribed, and both Mary Ann and her mother were arrested.

A post-mortem was called for and the baby's medicines were taken away. The examination showed various contradictory factors, one of which was the presence of a small amount of arsenic that had caused damage to her stomach. The relatives had no access to arsenic but it was revealed that in the dispensary at Mr Woolmer's, arsenic was on the shelf above the one holding the magnesia. The possibility of confusing them was refuted.

A lecturer in chemistry, Julian Edward Disbrowe Rodgers, carried out tests and concluded that a small degree of arsenic in the stomach might have caused a 'locked' bowel. After the post-mortem, however, the verdict was that the damage to the bowel would have happened before any administration of arsenic and, therefore, its presence or otherwise would not have caused the intussusception that was responsible for the baby's death.

Mary Ann Dore and her mother, Mary Spry, were forced to sit through this gruelling account of the little one's death. All those called to give evidence swore that as parent and grandparent, the two women had been loving and responsible carers for the small child. In the absence of any evidence to the contrary, they were found not guilty.

Chapter Nine

The Long Arm
of the Law

Keeping on the Straight and Narrow

Until the nineteenth century, the wellbeing of Island society was overseen by four appointed officers: the Churchwarden, the Overseer of the Poor, the Overseer of Highways, the Parish Constable. The Parish Constable was the backbone of local justice, the post going as far back as the role of the Saxon Tythingmen.

The job was unpopular and unpaid but those appointed were expected to serve for a year. To avoid this, men sometimes bribed or coerced others into taking their place.

The role of the Parish Constable was to oversee the night watchman, who was, in turn, appointed by a Watch Committee – made up of local businessmen. The Parish Constable would investigate offences, issue summonses and execute warrants, organise the hue and cry, take charge of prisoners, and obey the Orders of the Justices.

Recourse to the law could be had at the Petty Sessions, which have now evolved into the magistrates' courts. The Quarter Sessions were presided over by a Justice of the Peace; this would be a local bigwig – often lord of the manor – and frequently an MP. As such, he was expected to be able to mete out justice impartially.

The Crown Court dealt with the most serious crimes and was usually held twice a year, at which time a presiding judge would visit as part of his circuit. The Crown Court covering the Island traditionally met at Winchester.

Prisons were primarily seen not as places to send the guilty to serve out a sentence, but as a holding point until a punishment could be meted out. One punishment was branding on the cheek, carried out as an alternative to prison. The procedure often took place at the end of a case and in front of a jury. The victim would be branded with 'T' for thief or 'F' for felon. Sometimes branding was on the thumb. The last case recorded at the Old Bailey was in 1789 and the practice was abolished in 1829.

Hanging was another common punishment. Until 1783, the usual method of hanging was to place the guilty man on a cart, suspend a rope over the gallows and then drive the cart away, leaving him suspended. In 1783, the 'sharp drop' was introduced, whereby the offender fell through a trap, thus increasing the impact and hastening the end. The habit of displaying a hanged man in chains was discontinued after 1834. The last public hanging took place in 1868, and the last ever hanging was in 1964.

Burning at the stake continued until 1790, to be replaced by hanging and drawing, although women continued to be burned for the act of murdering their husbands. In 1820, the last case of hanging, drawing and quartering took place, following the Cato Street Conspiracy. The death penalty was abolished in England in 1969, but not in Ireland.

Other punishments were phased out at different times: birching/flogging was abolished in 1948, although it was still in use in prisons until 1962; caning, although prohibited in schools, was still legal until its total abolition in 1999; hard labour finished in 1948; the hulks were abandoned in 1857; the pillories were abolished in 1837; the stocks in 1872; and the treadmill in 1898.

Transportation

Transportation to America started in the sixteenth century and, initially, merchants transported the miscreants at their own expense, then sold their labour. Transportation to Australia began in 1787, only twelve years after the colony was discovered. It ceased in 1868. By this time, 160,000 men women and children had been forcibly removed from British shores.

Police

In 1829, Sir Robert Peel, as the Home Secretary, instigated the founding of the Metropolitan Police Act. In 1832, Winchester City Council followed suit and in 1837, the Isle of Wight Constabulary was established. Police officers were paid, wore uniforms and were provided with police houses – although deductions were taken from their pay for their upkeep. On duty, they wore white gloves and were admonished for smoking in public. The biggest cause of dismissal was drunkenness, and particular attention was paid to their behaviour on paydays.

In 1838, the old watch house at Newport was converted into a lock-up for men, while opposite, a butcher's shop was acquired in which to incarcerate women. The town clerk's office became the base for the super-intendent.

By 1852, the old bride-well in Holyrood Street was transformed into a police station and by 1869, a state-of-the-art station was built in Quay Street, complete with cells. In 1862, there were four sergeants operating from West Cowes, Yarmouth, Ventnor and Ryde. In the ensuing years, stations opened at Cowes, Sandown and, finally, Shanklin.

Recruiting was a problem. A candidate had to be physically fit and able to read and write. Like the Parish Constables of old, policemen were, at best, regarded with suspicion. As a result of low applications, East Cowes was served with one constable who was responsible for 3,000 residents. Consequently, he was on duty day and night. Sergeants were regularly admonished for failing to check on the watchmen during the night. In 1854, the familiar pocket book and pencil were issued. Officers were strictly forbidden to use them for anything other than official business.

'Well madam, I have to take down your particulars.'

Evading the Noose

In 1255, a man held in Countess Isabella's prison at Carisbrooke, on a charge of having killed one Ivo Urry, escaped and sought refuge in Godshill church. This form of sanctuary was recognised for forty days. The accused, William Bold, might have chosen to 'abjure the realm', in effect outlawing himself and leaving the country, but in this case he apparently chose to be tried, although the outcome is not recorded.

At this time, the Island was divided into two hundreds called the East and West Medine. When a suspicious death was discovered, the hue and cry was raised and somebody was despatched to inform the coroner. A jury was then summoned and twelve men from the Medine were called upon to attend the inquest. The types of case seen by the coroner have barely changed in 600

'Desist! He claims sanctuary!'

years. Drowning occurred with distressing regularity, bodies often being washed ashore never to be identified. Children frequently suffered accidents, drowned, were scalded or burned. Cases of manslaughter and murder were perhaps more frequent then than now. The most common cause of death, however, was 'visitation of God', meaning that the deceased died of natural causes.

The coroner was primarily concerned with how much money was at stake. Who committed a crime or how they were punished was of less interest than the haul of goodies at the end. Hence, the fate of most criminals of the time goes unrecorded. Some nineteenth-century records of Island inquests do still survive though. The details are often sketchy, but a record of the expense incurred was meticulously written down.

The average costs recorded for an 'inquisition' into a death usually included such items as:

The inquest: £1 6s 8d
The jury: 13s
Witnesses: 2s
Surgeon: £1 1s
Hire of a room: 2s 6d
To the person finding and taking care of the body: 5s
Transport in miles, average cost incurred: 5s

Frequently there was very little evidence as to what happened. Extracts from the Coroner's Book reveal some details of the sorts of cases that were taken up.

1851
James Morris of West Cowes. Verdict: manslaughter by persons unknown.
Frederick Cole of Ryde. Verdict: manslaughter against diverse persons unknown.
Henry Ryall at Goldings, aged forty-three. Verdict: hanged himself.
Michael Connel, aged twenty-one, at Parkhurst Barracks. Verdict: shot himself but not enough evidence to decide if he was of unsound mind (cost £2 7s 5d).

1854

Maurice Kennedy at Sconce Point Freshwater. Died from excessive drinking.

1855

Louis Rever at Parkhurst, aged twenty-three. Died from rupture of the spleen 'occasioned by excitement and passion'.
Anna Buckett, aged seventy-eight. Killed by a cart – accidental death.
John Holder Strange, aged forty-five – accidental fall from a cliff.

1858

Eleanor D'Esterre of East Cowes, aged seventy-eight – accidentally poisoned.

1862

Edward John Tuttiett of Newport, sixteen. Verdict: 'The deceased died form administering himself medicine to which he had incautiously added an undue proportion of hydrochloric acid.'

1863

Henry Slade at East Medina Mill, aged twenty-two – accidentally killed by the machinery of the mill.

The Court of Requests

This was a minor court meeting, held regularly to decide on cases of small debts. Established in 1483, it was thought to have died a natural death by the time of the English Civil War, but it was never formally abolished and was still operating on the Isle of Wight in the nineteenth century.

In 1836, the Court of Requests was held weekly at Newport and extended its jurisdiction over the entire Island. It had power to imprison people for debt – one day for each 1s owed. However, according to parliamentary papers, 'The number taken is very small in proportion to the number of suitors.' It dealt with debts of up to 40s and covered thirty parishes. Payments were sometimes by instalment, or goods could be confiscated to cover the debt. Sample cases from 1816 include:

29 July 1816

Dr Watermouth, a Newport surgeon, was to become famous for identifying the chalybeate spring at Niton as having health-giving qualities. It became a regular watering place with a grotto and the construction of the Royal Sandrock Hotel, the epithet royal being added after the future Queen Victoria visited. Dr Watermouth was primarily a physician, however, and in total he brought twenty-one cases for non payment of fees for medicines and visits to patients. In total he was owed £65 0s 10d in unpaid fees.

19 August 1816

John Saunders sued a total of thirty-four persons for non payment of debts

Crimes Committed on the Island

The Petty and Quarter Sessions covered most crimes perpetrated on the Island, although the most serious offences were transferred to Winchester and dealt with by the Crown Court.

Samples from the Isle of Wight Quarter Sessions of Easter 1836 include:

James Legg, late of Newport, indicted for stealing two cheeses at 20lbs weight from Joseph and Frederick Cowdery.

William Weeks, late of Newport, labourer, was accused that between 3 December 1835 and 13 March 1836, he embezzled several sums of money from his employer, Robert John Jewell. Held was in custody until 12 April 1836

'Serious' Crimes Dealt With through the Ages

23 April 1734
William Derrick was arrested for swearing ten oaths. His punishment was to be in the stocks for two hours, having refused to pay 10s.

6 July 1752
Thomas Traphill, a chapman of Newport, and John Clapp, for being drunk and disorderly.

20 August 1752
Thomas Derrick of Newport, for being drunk and disorderly.

22 October 1788
William Bannister for obstructing, hindering and molesting William Miller, workman, from making a cesspool and drain in front of Bannister's house, contrary to the Act for Paving, Repairing, Clearing Lighting and Watching the Streets of the Borough of Newport.

5 May 1796
Benjamin Stephens of Arreton, corn dealer, for falsifying returns to the Inspector of Corn Returns.

21 October 1815
Thomas Bolton, the younger of Newport, for deserting his wife, leaving her chargeable to the parish, being a vagabond and a rogue. Prosecutor William Allen, constable. Witness, Edward. Wavell, overseer of Newport. Bolton was committed to the House of Correction.

18 February 1817
George Plumbley sent to House of Correction for failing to support his wife and children.

10 April 1832
Order for the transportation for seven years of John Cockram, aged thirty-nine, of Newport, labourer and rag gatherer, for theft

by force of arms of 15lbs of copper, value at 5s, the goods and chattels of the crown. Cockram was recorded as married but with no children.

Other cases of transportation include:

William Fleming, aged forty, labourer of Newport, was sentenced to seven years' transportation for two charges of embezzling money from his employer, Hannah Denham, widow. Fleming was recorded as married with no children.

William Buckler of Newport, labourer, was sentenced to seven years' transportation for the theft with force of arms of a fowl, a dead fowl, 1lb of meat and feathers, property of William Paine.

George Gustar, eighteen, of Newport, labourer, was sentenced to be transported for the theft, with force and arms, of four shoes from Charles Lambert. Gustar was single and had a widowed mother renting a cottage near West Cowes. The prisoner was placed on board the prison hulk *York* in Portsmouth Harbour.

Being a Nuisance

31 March 1776
Jonathan Hennen, late of Newport, was prosecuted for unlawfully setting up a smith's shop, which was dangerous and improper for carrying the business of a smith. He also caused a nuisance by lighting fires and making a noise at unreasonable hours.

1 Oct 1777
William Ballard of Newport, mariner, caused a nuisance by allowing quantities of dung and other filth to run out from his hog sty into the highway near the Quay.

1783/4
James Gould, butcher, similarly caused a nuisance by leaving entrails and other filth from calves, sheep and lambs in the highway.

1820
Easter sessions. Hezikiah Cantelo, late of Newport, labourer, causing a nuisance by placing a quantity of dung and other filth in Chain Lane.

Thou Shalt Not Steal

1826
Epiphany session. Jens Jensen Beren, late of Newport, labourer, stole 2lbs of butter from Frederick Gottlieb Gayer.

1826
Easter Session. George Drayton, Joseph Clarke, George Taylor, William Goodwin, and James Jackson, labourers late of Newport, stole 600lbs of coffee and four canvas bags belonging to Samuel Smith Barber and James Finnie. They were all held in custody.

Knocking Down the Lock-Up

In 1907, there was no shortage of contractors queuing up to knock down Newport's old bridewell, the lock-up that had held local miscreants for several centuries. The old prison lay between the bottom of Holyrood Street and Crocker Street in Newport. In 1907, the site was purchased by brewers Mew Langton, to extend their premises and erect a new, state of the art malt house. In its turn, the brewery met a similar fate and the land is now occupied by Malthouse Court, which offers sheltered accommodation.

The 1851 and 1861, censuses both record Inspector George Grapes as the Superintendent of Police in Newport. He was living in Holyrood Street along with his wife, his unmarried sister, four daughters and a son. His son William did not follow him into the police service; instead he became an ironmonger's assistant. George was born in Newport and his wife, Anne Marie, came from Arreton. George died in 1879 at the age of seventy-five.

Chapter Ten

Miscellany

At Her Majesty's Pleasure

The death in 1892 of Prince Albert Victor, Duke of Clarence and Avondale, second in line to the British throne, was a gift to conspiracy theorists. Prince 'Eddie' had recently become engaged to Mary of Teck and was about to be made Viceroy of Ireland when an attack of influenza carried him off only weeks after his twenty-eighth birthday. One rumour was that he had died of syphilis; another that he had been poisoned. There was even speculation that he was Jack the Ripper. He was reported to frequent male brothels and also to have fathered a child while in India. One of the more dramatic tales was that he had been pushed off a cliff by Lord Randolph Churchill.

There were also those who insisted that he was not dead, but that he had been secretly removed to an asylum in the Isle of Wight. Mary of Tek, unwilling to let the chance of a crown pass her by, promptly became engaged to Eddie's younger brother, the future George V.

Ivory

The *Isle of Wight Observer* of 1861 records that William Robert Fletcher, a mariner, was to be charged with stealing two elephant tusks from a schooner, *Isabel*, docked at Cowes. The case was heard the following Monday.

The theft of two elephant tusks.

A Case of Crowded Bedroom

In May 1880, the *Isle of Wight Observer* reported that James Matthews, blacksmith of Arreton, was summoned for the offence of 'crowded bedroom'. Matthews, his wife and five children all shared a bedroom measuring 13ft square. This was considered by the Medical Officer of Health, Dr Foster, to be injurious to health because of insufficient air. He added that were it not for the extreme cleanliness of Mrs Matthews, the family would have suffered 'extreme consequences'. The Matthews family lived in a one-up one-down cottage at Heasley Farm, where James worked.

Was He Pushed or did He Dive in Head First?

In the nineteenth century, Ryde blossomed from a remote fishing village into a fashionable seaside resort. It was a great place for pubs. In 1865, John Cooper, a local brewer with premises off Union Street, was found dead in one of his own barrels of beer. How he came to be inside the barrel was a mystery. Equally taxing was the question of how to get him out, as he was securely jammed. Eventually, the barrel was dragged out into the lane and broken open with sledgehammers. A crowd gathered around armed with jugs and bowls, and as the first liquid gushed into the street, they rushed forward to collect it. Beer, even with added body, was too good to waste. As there was no evidence as to how John met his end, no one was charged with his murder.

Unhappy at Work

The *Isle of Wight Times* of 7 May 1863 reported that John Drudge of Dodnor Farm accused his apprentice, George Prince, of neglecting his work and using abusive language. Prince was consigned to prison for one month with hard labour and was to lose one month's wages. He was then to return to his master.

Similarly, the *Salisbury and Winchester Journal* warned that Benjamin Young, apprentice to a carpenter and joiner at Newport, had run away. He was described as twenty years of age, about 5ft 5in in height, and rather thickset. The newspaper warned, 'This is to caution all persons not to employ or harbour the said apprentice as they will be prosecuted for the same.'

Slow Down!

In 1893, American Inventor Henry House acquired premises in East Cowes, in which to perfect the use of liquid gas as a fuel. He was not without supporters, for Edward Prince of Wales, his younger brother, Prince Leopold, his uncle, Leopold (King of the Belgians), and his wealthy friend, Thomas Lipton, all took an avid interest. Unfortunately, the locals were appalled by the speed at which his vehicle raced down York Avenue, right past the entrance to Osborne House. He was prosecuted and fined £3 plus costs. Infuriated that Islanders failed to appreciate the arrival of the motor car, he returned to the mainland depriving 200 local people of their jobs. His myriad ventures included paper plates, sand-blasting, a phonetic telegraph, a knitting machine and, perhaps most enduring – shredded wheat!

A Tale from the Newgate Calendar

On 21 March 1797, Gaspard Koep and Nicholas Wagner were accused of the violent assault and rape of Elizabeth, wife of Richard Lock, of Claybrook Common in Whippingham Parish. The trial took place at the Winchester Assizes, where sixty-four other men were also on trial for their crimes. Koep and Wagner were both sentenced to death, along with twelve others, .

Shoot Out at the Institute

In spring 1901, there was a growing interest in the lectures taking place at Shanklin Institute. It was not so much driven by a desire for knowledge, as by a longing to know what would happen next. What did happen must have surpassed the most outlandish imagination.

Victor Michael Ruthen, a former monk who had left the Catholic Church with some animosity, now made it his mission to expose the perceived iniquities of his former calling. To this end, he hired the Shanklin Institute (now known as Shanklin Theatre/Town Hall) to deliver a series of lectures.

Over the weeks, as the word spread, the audience grew and on Sunday 3 March, Ruthven chose as his theme 'the secret dealings between women and priests in the confessional'. A previous lecture had been advertised as 'Rome the ruin of nations', and the local priest, Father Bom, had successfully prosecuted Ruthven for libel.

Undeterred, Ruthven took the stage to face an excited audience. Such was the uproar that he had difficulty in making himself heard. Present was a particularly vociferous man named Jones. The pair had crossed swords before and when Jones threw his cap at Ruthven, the lecturer moved to the front of the stage and began to brandish a pistol.

Faced with a riot, Ruthven retreated down some stairs at the back of the auditorium, to be followed by William Wadham a fishmonger's assistant. Wadham intended to take the pistol from Ruthven but the latter fired, wounding him. Wadham then staggered towards the stairs before collapsing. Ruthven, who had managed to open the outer door, went outside but was grabbed by the arm. The pistol was taken from him.

Ruthven now appeared in court accused of shooting William Wadham, with intent to kill. Evidence was given by Mr Wadham and others. Numerous witnesses were called and Ruthven pleaded not guilty, his defence being that he was afraid of the howling mob and had fired a shot solely to defend himself. In the event, he was found guilty but only sentenced to nine months in prison.

A case of self defence?

Select Bibliography

Books

Bebbington, G., *A Brief Life: Being the Story of John Valentine Gray, A Climbing Boy*, County Press, 1990

Brettell, T., *A Topographical and Historical Guide to the Isle of Wight*, Leight & Co., 1840

Hockey, S.F., *Insula Vecta: the Isle of Wight in the Middle Ages*, Phillimore, 1982

Manser, B., *Behind the Small Wooden Door*, Coach House Publications, 2000

McKie, D., *Jabez: The Rise and Fall of a Victorian Rogue*, Atlantic, 2004

Watt, I.A., *A History of the Hampshire and Isle of Wight Constabulary 1839–1966*, Phillimore, 2006

Newspapers

Hampshire Chronicle
Isle of Wight County Press
Isle of Wight Observer

Journals & Records

Old Bailey records online
Salisbury and Winchester Journal
Stroud, A. (ed.), *Yesterday's Papers* (5 Volumes), extracts from the *Isle of Wight County Press*